High-Performance Handling Handbook

DON ALEXANDER

MBI Publishing Company

First published in 2002 by MBI Publishing Company, Galtier Plaza, Suite 200, 380 Jackson Street, St. Paul, MN 55101-3885 USA

MBI Publishing Company books are also available at discounts in bulk quantity for industrial or sales-promotional use. For details write to Special Sales Manager at Motorbooks International Wholesalers & Distributors, Galtier Plaza, Suite 200, 380 Jackson Street, St. Paul, MN 55101-3885 USA.

Library of Congress Cataloging-in-Publication Data Available

ISBN: 0-7603-0948-5

Printed in the United States of America

On the front cover: Even cars that handle well from the factory, such as this Honda Prelude, can be improved through careful, well-reasoned modifications. *James Brown*

On the back cover: (top) This Ford touring car makes the most of its stiff suspension and aerodynamic add-ons. *Ford Motorsports UK*

(lower left) This device is one of the more accurate ways to measure the toe setting when aligning a race car. *Advanced Racing Technologies*

(lower right) Taking a tire's temperature reveals much about how the rubber is interacting with the road surface.

Contents

Acknowledgments

Jeff Cheechov, Progress Group
Jonathan Speigel, Progress Group
Greg Woo, Neuspeed
Bill Neumann, Neuspeed
Roland Graef, H & R Springs
Earl Knoper, Toyo Tires
Mary Jo Thomas, Aras Group (Yokohama Tires)
Shari McCullough-Arfons, McCullough Public Relations (Continental/General Tires)
Mariellen Fagen, McCullough Public Relations (Continental/General Tires)
John Rastetter, Tire Rack
Dave Hudrlik, Kumho Tires
Rick Brennan, Kumho Tires

Ralph Hollack, Autotech Sport Tuning (Zender Wheels)
Athene Karis, Karis Communications (BF Goodrich Tires)
Tanya Oxford Energy Suspension
Don, Autopower
John Lewis, Panoz Racing School
John Hotchkis, Hotchkis Tuning
Doug Burke, Wildwood Brakes
Gary Peek, Eibach Springs
Mark Richter, Yokohama Tires
Jennifer Gerber, Audi North America
Mike Whelan, Subaru USA
Bruce Foss, Hoosier Tires
Sheldon Tackett, M/C Tech Motorsports
Jeff Donker, Holland Communications
Rick Herrick

George Crezee
Hal Parker
Chris Bly, Franczak Enterprises
Lionel Best, Franczak Enterprises
Bill Bainbridge
Jim Hodgman, Brembo Brakes
Mike Saeva
Danny McKeever, Fastlane Racing School
Allison McKeever, Fastlane Racing School
Jay Morris, Ground Control
Ron Wood, VW Specialties
James Brown, James Brown Photography
Christie Helm, test driver
Ryan Flaherty

Introduction

Cornering power! Braking power! Acceleration! Four little patches of rubber provide the traction needed to accomplish each of these actions. Handling performance is about improving the traction needed to do each of these. It takes suspension parts, springs, shocks, antiroll bars, tires, wheels, and tuning to make significant improvements. Today, getting a street-driven vehicle to corner in excess of 1.0 gs cornering force is doable but not easy. Every component must work together perfectly. Components must be suited not only to the car but to

each other, and they must be tuned to work together flawlessly. Just installing bigger tires and wheels will not get you far. In many cases, a suspension system where the components fail to work in unison is one that actually hurts performance. But there is nothing more fun than driving a car that is right. Everything works together, creating a car that sticks to the road and is completely responsive to every driver control input. Balance is neutral and grip is scary fast. The feeling generates adrenaline and confidence at the same time.

Compared to getting more engine power, increasing handling performance is a major task. It's not necessarily more work, but it does require more knowledge. It's a significant task because so many factors come into play. The good news is that most of the work today is accomplished by the tire companies and the suspension component manufacturers. Many of today's products provide excellent performance because the products are both well-engineered and thoroughly tested on a test track.

Section I
Tuning for Maximum Performance

The first section of *High-Performance Handling Handbook* reveals the basic principles of handling and covers each component part of the suspension system. Vehicle dynamics, suspension components, and tire traction are covered in detail. Specific systems are explained so that you can understand how systems work and what changes can be made and what products are available to improve handling performance. There are chapters covering testing, tuning, handling, and motorsports. As you read this section, several factors should be kept in mind.

First, to understand handling and how to improve it you need a basic understanding of vehicle dynamics. That is why the vehicle dynamics chapter is early in the book. Next, you need to know what is possible and what is available to improve performance. Finally, understanding how to tune the suspension components, starting with a basic alignment, makes all the difference in performance. You can start with the best components, the stickiest tires, and the right look, but without tuning the suspension to fit the parts and the conditions, you will get a degraded performance. Tuning correctly is crucial for any type of competition or track-day participation, but it's also necessary for street driving, though to a lesser degree.

All information in this book is general and may relate to the handling and suspension of street-driven vehicles or cars used on the track. Information is presented so that you can make decisions and compromises that best suit your individual needs. Use the information accordingly. The compromises you make will affect the handling and performance of your car. If you follow the guidelines, you will improve safety as well. The flip side of making decisions that improve performance is increased discomfort. If you are modifying a car for competition only, the choices are easy. For the street, you can make a car so uncomfortable that it is no longer fun to drive. In general, improved handling performance means a harsher ride, more road noise, more vibration, less ground clearance, and accelerated component wear, especially tires. The stiffer you make everything, the more true this becomes. There is always a temptation to push the envelope to improve handling on the street. Going too far is costly and takes the fun out of driving your car. So be prudent.

If you are building a dual-purpose vehicle for track days, autocrossing, or drag racing, you will have to live with some compromises that make street driving less enjoyable. You can easily swap some components, such as wheels and tires, and change ride heights shock absorber settings to improve the situation, but the comfort level on the street will deteriorate as the modifications become more extensive.

The overriding goal of this section of *High-Performance Handling Handbook* is to give you the knowledge and information to create the level of handling performance you desire for your vehicle, thereby increasing the fun factor.

The information in this book is intended to educate and provide an overview of handling and how to improve it. Consult with manufacturers, dealers, installation centers, and factory repair manuals for specific information on a given car or truck. If you do not possess the tools and skills to install and tune suspension components, find someone to do it for you. If you do it yourself, always use jack stands under the vehicle and exercise extreme caution when working with springs. Do not remove springs without completely reading installation instructions from the manufacturer and in a factory repair manual, and use a good spring compressor. The motorsports overview is intended to give you an idea of what you can do with your vehicle. Contact the various associations for specific information and safety rules.

Improving handling performance improves the safety of your car. It will also make it faster, so use caution and good judgment when you drive. And please be courteous to other drivers who may not have the driving skills or a vehicle with the performance you possess.

Chapter One
What Is Handling?

Improved performance, improved feel, and the right look characterize good handling. On the road, feel and looks are a higher priority. For motorsports applications, performance comes first. *James Brown*

How often have you heard the phrase "good handling"? Just what is that? For many drivers, good handling is a feeling. Some describe it as improved responsiveness. While that is part of the equation, good handling encompasses much more than just feel or responsiveness. Good handling means more traction during braking, cornering, and acceleration, quicker response to driver control inputs, good balance at the limit, and, in competition, lower elapsed times or faster lap times.

A car that handles well has three primary characteristics. First, it makes the best possible use of the tires' traction capacity. Second, it has a good balance of traction front to rear. Third, it is instantly responsive to the driver's steering, brake, and throttle inputs.

Maximum traction implies sticky tires, but sticky tires only aid traction when they have good contact with the road. What keeps the four tire contact patches on the road surface is a combination of tire sidewall stiffness, suspension geometry, the ability of the springs and shocks to control the tires over bumps, the degree of roll resistance offered by the antiroll bars and springs, and the compliance of the suspension bushings. Thus, good traction requires far more than wider rims and a new set of tires.

Superior handling incorporates handling balance, a problem that confronts even top race drivers. Most

Improved braking is part of the package. Testing performance modifications is a key factor in finding superior braking. *Jeff Cheechov*

everyone has heard the terms *push* or *loose* in TV race coverage. A push, or understeer, means the front tires lose traction before the rear. The car will not turn as much as it should as the limits of tire traction are reached. A loose condition, or oversteer, means the rear tires lose traction before the front tires. Thus, the car will turn more than it should as the tires reach the limits of traction. The biggest influence on handling balance is the balance in roll resistance of the front springs and antiroll bar compared to the rear springs and antiroll bar. If you take a car with neutral handling and stiffen the rear antiroll bar or springs, the car may become loose, or oversteer. If you stiffen the front springs or bars instead, the car may push or understeer. The job of the aftermarket spring and antiroll bar is to control body roll and create the optimum balance between front and rear roll resistance so that the handling balance is near neutral.

Responsiveness to driver control inputs is the third characteristic of good handling. While stiffer springs and antiroll bars, stiffer suspension bushings, and stiffer, short tire sidewalls all improve a car's responsiveness, the biggest influence here is the shock absorber. Stiffer shocks improve responsiveness, to a point. Shocks that are too stiff will make the car twitchy to drive and cause it to skate over bumps, actually hurting traction and overall handling performance.

A well-conceived suspension system addresses all of these factors and uses suspension components that are compatible with the car, the driving and road conditions, and the degree of desired handling performance. Ill-conceived systems can hurt cornering and overall handling performance and deteriorate ride quality as well. Let's

Skid pad testing determines the cornering power of the tires. Suspension modifications are made to improve the compliance of the tire contact patch on the road surface, as shown on this modified front-wheel-drive Honda Civic. *Rick Herrick*

This bare 1964 Chevelle chassis from Hotchkis Performance shows suspension modifications including wheels, tires, springs, shocks, antiroll bars, bushings, and suspension control arms. *Hotchkis Tuning*

take a look at the factors and components that must be right to achieve good handling.

Tire Loads

When a car is at rest, a certain amount of weight rests on each tire contact patch. This static weight distribution influences the traction at each corner of the car. The traction of a tire is proportional to the weight, or load, on the tire contact patch. If the load increases, the traction increases; if the load decreases, the traction decreases. The relationship is non-linear, however. This means that if the load is doubled on a tire, the traction is something

less than double. We'll look at this in more detail in the next chapter.

Weight Transfer

When a car accelerates, brakes, or corners, some portion of the weight or vertical load will effectively transfer from front to rear, rear to front, or inside to outside. This changes the traction at each tire contact patch. For a given car and rate of acceleration, slowing, or cornering, a given amount of weight will transfer from one set of tires (front, rear, left, or right) to the opposite set of tires. What effect this has on handling depends on where the weight is transferred, when it's

transferred, and how fast it gets there.

Weight moves from the front to the rear under acceleration, from the rear to the front under braking, and from the inside to the outside while cornering. But while cornering, some of the weight moves to the front outside and some moves to the rear outside. The comparative stiffness of the springs and antiroll bars (roll resistance) between the front and rear determines how much weight moves to the outside front versus the outside rear. If a spring or antiroll bar is stiffer at one end of the car, that end of the car will get more of the sideways weight transfer during cornering. That end of the car will also have less traction relative to the other end of the car. For example, stiffening the front springs or antiroll bars will cause more weight to transfer to the outside front and cause more understeer or push (or reduce oversteer). Antiroll bars and springs rates are used to control this handling balance.

When the weight transfer occurs depends on when the driver uses the controls and how quickly those controls are moved. Abrupt use of the controls —steering, throttle, brake, gearshift—can cause abrupt weight transfer, upsetting the handling balance and deteriorating handling quality.

Compliance in the suspension system determines how quickly weight is transferred. The major component here is the shock absorber, though sus-

Overall handling performance is best evaluated on a slalom course, which tests the extremes of transient handling response. *Rick Herrick*

To improve performance, tire loads are critical. The goal is to have equal tire loads at each corner of the car while turning. This front-drive car, a Renault Clio racing at Silverstone, England, has lifted the inside front tire, which is now unable to provide traction for either cornering or acceleration exiting the corner. This is not desirable on a front-drive racecar and is caused by a front anitroll bar that is too stiff for conditions.

This Honda del Sol has aftermarket wheels and tires, but the suspension is stock.

Here the del Sol has modified suspension. The lower ride height improves performance, feel, and looks. *Jeff Cheechov*

pension bushings play a small role. Stiffer shocks cause weight to move faster. Softer shocks cause weight to move slower. As mentioned above, increasing shock stiffness improves handling to a point, after which the tires will lose contact with the road surface on bumpy stretches. Stiffer shocks (combined with stiffer springs) also reduce ride comfort.

Tire Pressure

Tire pressures affect the shape of the tire contact patch, which affects the load across the tread of the tire. If a tire is overinflated, the center of the contact patch is loaded more than the edges of the patch. Underinflation has the opposite effect. Finding the optimum tire pressure for the car, tires, wheels, and suspension system ensures that each contact patch is evenly loaded and maximum traction is available.

Camber

Camber is the tilt of a tire when viewed from the front (or rear) of the car. Camber is positive if the top of the tire is tilted to the outside and negative if the tilt is to the inside. Since most suspension systems gain positive camber during bump (compression) travel, and the outside tire goes into bump during cornering, some amount of negative camber is needed to offset the camber gain and keep the tire contact patch flat on the road surface during cornering.

Camber gain is caused by suspension geometry changes caused by body roll. During body roll the outside front tire (usually) gains camber. This tilts the tire contact patch and changes the loading across the tread, reducing traction. Some static negative camber can compensate for this, but too much negative camber causes accelerated tire wear and hurts straight-line braking performance. Stiffer front springs and antiroll bars reduce body roll, which reduces bump travel and camber gain. This reduces the amount

Look at the steering angle of the front wheels and tires. The greater wheel angle of the car on the left indicates that understeer is present, while the car on the right with less wheel angle indicates a neutral handling balance.

of static negative camber needed to keep the tire contact patch flat on the road surface in a corner.

Toe

Toe is the angle of the front tires when viewed from above. Toe-in means the fronts of the tires are closer together than the rear of the tires. Toe-out is the opposite. Cars will turn into a corner better with a small amount of toe-out. Toe-in offers more stability in a straight-line, so for highway and daily street driving, a small amount of toe-in is preferred. Too much toe-in or toe-out will increase tire wear. Rear suspensions can also have toe-in or toe-out. Some cars actually work better with a small amount of toe-out at the rear, but most cars need some toe-in at the rear to ensure straight-line stability, especially for drag racing or high-speed road courses.

The del Sol with stock suspension shows a high degree of body roll. Note the excessive camber angle on the outside front tire at the contact patch. This reduces cornering force, increases tire wear, and hurts performance.

Here the del Sol corners much flatter with less camber change and more tire traction. Stiffer springs and antiroll bars reduce the body roll. *Jeff Cheechov*

Here is a good example of reduced body roll on the skid pad. This Honda Civic Si will corner at much higher speeds with the suspension modifications. *Jeff Donker*

These front suspension systems from Formula One cars show the progression in leading-edge suspension design. The inboard suspension from a 1970's Ferrari (top) is much more sophisticated than the outboard suspension from the '60's grand prix car.

Caster

Caster is the angle of the steering axis at the front of the car when viewed from the side (see illustration). More caster increases the self-centering effect of the steering, but also increases tire scrub slightly while cornering. Different caster angles on the left and right side cause the steering to pull in one direction. Using the factory-recommended caster angle is preferred.

Ride Height

Lowering a car reduces weight transfer and improves cornering performance by lowering the center of gravity. It also reduces suspension travel, so stiffer springs are needed to keep the car from bottoming out over bumps or bottoming on the suspension, which can cause damage, especially to shock absorbers.

Springs

The job of the springs is first to keep the car from bottoming; second, to allow the tire contact patches to stay on the road surface over bumps; and finally, to partially control body roll. Stiffer springs allow a car to have a lower ride height and also reduce body roll, both important for improved handling. On the other hand, stiffer springs reduce the ability of the tire contact patch to stay on the road surface over bumps, hurting traction on bumpy roads as well as increasing ride harshness. Any spring choice represents a compromise based on a driver's ride and handling priorities.

Antiroll Bars

Antiroll bars serve two purposes. First, as the name suggests, they control body roll so that camber gain is not excessive. Second, the bars are a convenient way to balance the roll resistance front to rear to achieve the best handling balance. Stiffer springs play a role in these functions but could not replace antiroll bars without being too stiff for comfort and control on bumpy surfaces.

Shocks

Shocks are designed to control spring movements over bumps. Without shocks, the springs would continue to oscillate, causing the car to bob down the road. In a performance application, shocks are used to control how fast weight is transferred and thus influence the responsiveness of the car to driver inputs. Shocks can be tuned in both bump (compression) and rebound travel and can operate at various shaft speeds to achieve a variety of handling characteristics under many road or track conditions. Shocks must be designed to work in a specific application to achieve good handling characteristics.

Bushings

Suspension bushings are intended to reduce and insulate the car's occupants from road noise and vibration. Bushings also permit the suspension to move through its arc of travel. Stock bushings are usually made of rubber. The soft rubber insulates well but allows a high degree of compliance in the suspension. This hinders responsiveness to driver inputs and increases suspension deflection, hurting overall handling performance. Solid metal

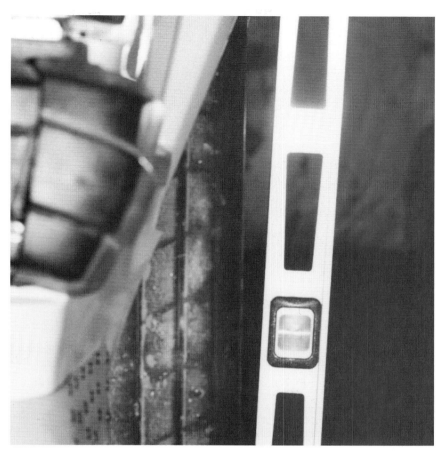

The front of this car shows negative camber. For motorsports the amount of camber should be equal to the amount of camber change and compliance in the tire/wheel so that the tire contact patch is flat on the road surface while cornering at the limit of tire traction. Here the negative camber is about 2 degrees.

After wheels and tires, the next step in improved handling performance is springs. This sport spring kit is from Eibach. *Eibach Springs*

bushings reduce compliance to nearly zero, but they are noisy and harsh. Urethane bushings reduce compliance considerably but maintain some comfort and noise control. Just adding performance bushings to your car will improve handling noticeably.

Chassis Bracing

A variety of chassis stiffeners and strut tower braces are available for many street and motorsports applications. By limiting chassis flex, such bracing reduces suspension movement, making the car more responsive and reducing handling issues such as camber change. When a chassis flexes, it acts like an undamped spring, which can be very difficult to control and tune. Chassis bracing improves handling but also makes the ride harsher.

Tuning

Even after installing a fully integrated suspension system consisting of springs, antiroll bars, shocks, bushings, wheels, and tires, the system needs to be tuned for optimum performance. At a minimum, the proper tire pressures and suspension alignment settings must be found. Tuning can make big improvements in handling performance once you have the best components on your car. It's also a broad subject, which is why a major part of this book is devoted to alignment and tuning. Even for the street, tuning pays significant dividends in improved performance and better tire wear. And the best-handling car is also the safest, since good handling and braking mean you have a better chance to avoid an impending accident.

Drive System Characteristics

While each type of drive system has its individual characteristics, the tire contact patches do not know what type of drive system they are trying to control. We do exactly the same things to a front driver that we do to a rear-or all-wheel-drive vehicle to get the handling balanced and maximum traction from the entire vehicle. Overall, the differences are more significant to driving technique than to drive system adjustments. There are a couple of exceptions.

First, the higher suspension frequency (determined by spring rate among other factors; see chapter 3) will go at the driven end of the vehicle with an all-wheel drive being treated as a front driver if the weight bias is to the front. Second, on a front-drive vehicle with more than about 59 percent of the weight on the front end, the rear roll stiffness should be high enough to unweight the inside rear tire contact patch considerably in a corner. On the track or autocross course, this usually means that the tire contact patch is just off the track surface. This is usually what is needed to counteract understeer, and it is accomplished with a stiffer antiroll bar. On the highway, a slightly softer setup is needed for stability. Beyond these specifics, we engineer and tune the

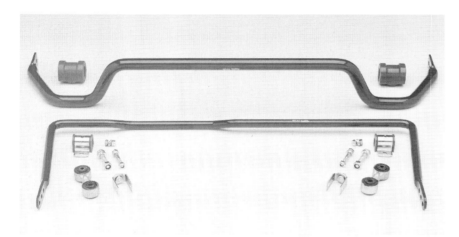

Antiroll bars won't help the looks but are crucial for performance. This front and rear antiroll bar package is from Eibach. *Eibach Springs*

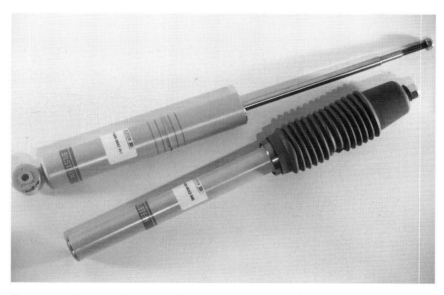

Shocks play a key role in both responsiveness and control of the tire contact patch. A good set of shocks, such as the front and rear Bilstein shocks shown here, is a crucial element of a complete handling package.

chassis in exactly the same way regardless of the drive system.

The Issues

There are two decisions that you must make when you begin the quest for improved handling. First, how will you use the car?

- Street or highway only?
- Combination of highway and motorsports?
- Competition only?

Second, what compromises must you make, or are you willing to make, to achieve improved handling? These will be different for each individual and for each of the above categories.

Street and Highway Applications

If you will use your car only on the street or highway, consider the following factors and their relative importance for you:

- Type of daily driving
- Fun driving (mountain roads, canyons, interstate ramps)
- Budget
- Importance of ride quality
- Desired (and practical) ground clearance
- Vehicle appearance
- Product availability for your vehicle
- Driving skills
- Mechanical skills

Combined Street and Motorsports Applications

If you plan to compete with your daily driver, consider the following factors:

- Type of event (drag race, autocross, rally, track days)
- Category of competition
- Rules
- Budget
- Product availability for your vehicle
- Ease of conversion from road to track specs (tires/wheels, ride height, alignment)

- Ride quality
- Ground clearance

Competition Only

This one is much easier. The compromises are geared toward making your vehicle as fast as possible. But you should still consider the following:

- Type of competition
- Suitability of your vehicle
- Class

- Budget
- Availability of parts for your vehicle
- Mechanical skills
- Driving skills

Your goals and desires, along with your budget, will settle most of your decisions. The rest is combining your parts and goals to achieve optimum performance. We will look at those issues in greater detail throughout the book.

Coil-over units (springs over shocks) with threaded adjusters for ride height make suspension fine-tuning easier and are great for vehicles used as daily drivers and for motorsports.

Suspension bushings improve responsiveness by reducing compliance. Polyurethane bushings as shown in this kit from Energy Suspension improve responsiveness without causing excessive noise and vibration. *Energy Suspension*

Chapter Two
Vehicle Dynamics and Suspension Modifications

Vehicle dynamics encompasses all of the forces that affect the performance of a car. These forces interact within a highly complex system as the car accelerates, brakes, and corners through a wide range of speeds and over varying surfaces and surface conditions. Understanding this system fully would take years, perhaps even a lifetime, of study. Fortunately, it's much easier to acquire a solid knowledge of the basics, and with this virtually any driver can greatly improve a car's handling.

For our purposes, we will focus on a competition setup, since it is easier to understand. For street performance, other parameters come into play, such as ride comfort, tire wear, budget, and how the car will be used. But for competition, all we care about is getting the car around (or down) the race track as quickly as possible. We want maximum acceleration, braking, and cornering force. That means finding the most traction possible within our performance parameters, whether it's for a single pass down a drag strip, one

Understanding vehicle dynamics is essential to controlling the tire contact patches for maximum traction during cornering, braking, and acceleration. *Jeff Donker*

The primary dynamic problem for a front-drive car is acceleration, both from a launch and exiting a corner. Weight transfer to the rear during acceleration reduces the load on the front tires and, hence, the traction at the front. *Jeff Donker*

run on an autocross course, or a 12-hour endurance road race.

It's comparatively easy to find maximum traction for acceleration in a straight-line, and the setup for max traction for a single lap or pass is much easier to find than the setup that allows the highest possible AVERAGE traction over a long event. We must find the best compromise between the often conflicting dynamics needs of cornering, braking, and accelerating. To do that, we need to consider not just each component of the system, but how these components interact.

Understanding Tire Traction

Most of us understand that tires make traction through friction between the rubber molecules at the tire contact patch and the road surface. And most of us understand that traction increases as vertical load on the tire increases, which is why aerodynamic downforce works so well. In addition, we understand that the tire will make more traction if the entire contact patch is equally loaded, which is why monitoring tire temperatures is useful. Within this basic knowledge are misconceptions and misinformation

that can add confusion to an already difficult topic. Let's try to shed some light on these ideas.

Let's start by considering the tire characteristics that affect traction. The following is the complete list:

• Basic tire design and construction
• Sidewall rigidity
• Tread rubber compound
• Tread design
• Tire size

Tire size, compound, and possibly tread design are the only choices we have, and those are limited. We can also control the following:

• Tire pressure
• Tire camber
• Tire toe-in (or -out)
• Camber change

Each of these parameters has an optimum setting that allows the tire to create maximum traction for a given set of circumstances on a given car. Then there is the vertical load on the tire, which is crucial to understand, but is also the most misunderstood element of tire traction. Traction increases as the vertical load on the tire increases, but the relationship is not linear. Traction does not increase as quickly as load, therefore each unit increase in load does not produce an equivalent increase in traction. This is a good time to look closely at traction in terms of pounds of force and vertical load on a tire.

One way to look at traction is in pounds of force. Most performance enthusiasts have heard the term g force,

All-wheel drive provides the ultimate traction for acceleration, especially in slippery road conditions. This Audi Quattro Trans-Am car dominated the 1988 Trans Am series with its superior traction. *Audi Sport North America*

This rear-drive Mustang GT has the advantage of weight transferring to the rear-drive wheels during acceleration.

Vertical load is the load actually seen at the tire contact patch. This includes the weight resting on the patch plus any aerodynamic downforce (or minus any aerodynamic lift). Aerodynamic downforce is great because it increases traction without increasing the weight of the car. Let's examine this more closely, since this is another area of some confusion.

Downforce is pretty much a traction freebie. It costs a little in acceleration at high speeds and reduces top speed somewhat, but it adds no weight to the car. That's important because added weight actually reduces the relative amount of traction compared to the total weight of the vehicle. Here's an example: Let's say a 3,000-pound car makes 3,000 pounds of cornering force at the limit with a given set of tires. That's 1.0 g of lateral force. Now let's add 500 pounds to the car without changing anything else. It's easy to understand that the car will not accelerate as quickly because it weighs more and the engine is making the same horsepower. It is less obvious that cornering speed will go down. Here's why. The 500 pounds of weight adds 500 pounds of vertical load to the tires, but because the relationship between the vertical load increase and traction increase is not linear, the amount of traction increase will only be about 400 pounds. That means the tires now

which is the force of gravity. If a car accelerates at 1.0 g, and the car weighs 3,000 pounds, then the tires are producing 3,000 pounds of traction force. This applies to acceleration forward, braking (negative acceleration), and cornering (lateral acceleration). A performance car considered to have good handling, such as a Z06 Corvette, can produce a cornering force of about 0.99 gs, braking force of about 1.01 gs, and somewhere around 0.50 gs accelerating in first gear. For a 3,500-pound car cornering at 0.99 gs, the traction in pounds is 3,465 pounds (3,500 x 0.99 = 3,465). That is a lot of force from those four tire contact patches. Put a DOT-rated R compound tire on the same car and the cornering force rises to 1.05 gs.

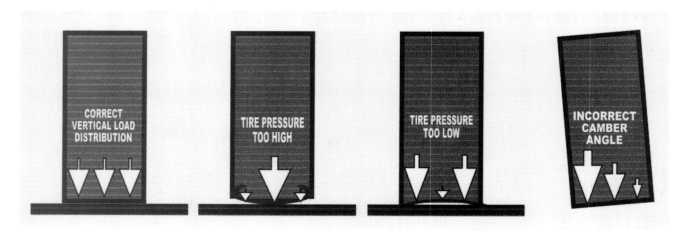

This illustration shows how vertical load is distributed at the tire contact patch under a variety of circumstances.

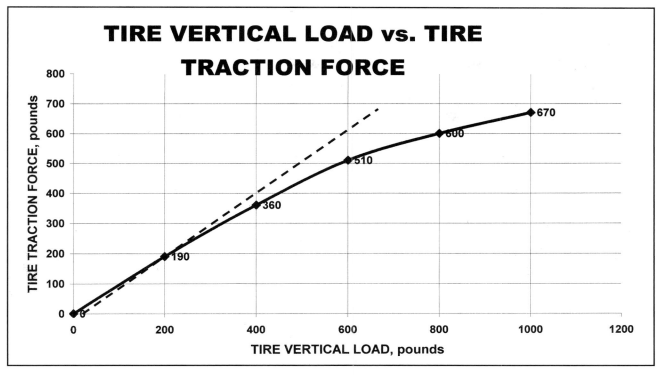

TIRE VERTICAL LOAD vs. TIRE TRACTION FORCE

The solid line on the graph shows typical tire traction force at several loads. The dashed line shows what a linear relationship would look like where tire traction force increases at the same rate as vertical load. The curve of the graph indicates that as vertical load increases, so does tire traction, but at a slower rate.

make an additional 400 pounds of traction, which means the cornering force of the car has dropped to 0.97 gs (3,400 pounds of traction for a 3,500-pound car). This nonlinear relationship also becomes more significant as the design load of the tire is approached. If a tire has a maximum load capacity of 2,000 pounds, but normally carries only 750 pounds, doubling the load to 1,500 is approaching the design limit. Here the traction may only increase by about half the extra load. If the design load is exceeded, the situation gets worse.

While there is nothing you can actually do to a tire or suspension to change this nonlinear relationship, there are plenty of factors you need to understand in order to minimize its effect and allow your car to create the maximum possible amount of traction.

The following factors are crucial to maximize traction for each individual tire:

- Camber angle at the front
- Camber at the rear for cars with independent or adjustable rear suspension
- Tire pressure at each tire
- Toe settings front and rear (axle or axle housing squareness on solid-axle cars)
- Roll steer and axle squareness at the rear
- Bump steer

Tire Contact Patch

A bigger tire contact patch, all else being equal, means more traction, but bigger is not always faster. Sometimes a wider tire is slower because it increases rolling resistance too much or because the suspension cannot control the tire contact patch effectively (camber change and so on). Whatever size tire you run, it is important to get as much of the tire contact patch working for you as you possibly can.

The uniform goal in every case is to have the vertical load exerted on the tire evenly distributed across the tire contact patch. If the entire contact patch is not equally loaded, you are not getting all the traction possible from that tire. If you look at the tire contact patch as a series of 1-inch squares, one

These illustrations show camber angles and their relationship to vertical.

CAMBER GAIN IN BUMP TRAVEL

Camber change occurs when the suspension travels into bump or rebound (up or down). This causes the tire contact patch to partially lose touch with the road surface unless travel is limited (including travel due to body roll) and static camber settings are changed from 0 to compensate. The goal is to have the tire contact patch equally loaded across the surface in a corner.

square compared to another acts just like one tire compared to another tire. Reducing the load on one square increases the load on another square. The square-losing load loses traction more quickly, and the other square gains traction from the increased load. Thus overall traction declines.

Once you have the entire tire contact patch at each corner working to its maximum traction potential, then the goal is to get all four tires creating the maximum amount of traction possible for the whole vehicle. To accomplish this requires an understanding of weight transfer. Many factors contribute to

traction, including construction characteristics, design, peak slip angles, and track conditions. The things controlled to some degree by the enthusiast, such as weight distribution and chassis setup, make all the difference in handling. In motorsports, the team making best use of the potential traction at all four tires is the team with the best chance to win.

Tire Slip Angle

When a car is going straight, the midline of the wheel and the midline of the tire contact patch are parallel. As the car begins to turn, this ceases to be

the case because the wheel is connected to the contact patch through the side-wall of the tire, which twists under cornering force. This twist allows the wheel to turn at a greater angle than the tire contact patch turns. The difference between the wheel centerline and the contact patch centerline in a turn is called the slip angle. As speeds increase the slip angle increases until it reaches a point of maximum cornering force. Below that angle, cornering force is less, and above it the tire will break free and slide.

Both front and rear tires produce slip angles during cornering. When they are equal, the car's handling balance is neutral. When they are bigger at the front than the rear, the car will push, or understeer. When they are greater at the rear, the car will be loose, or oversteer. The goal for the driver is to keep the tire at the optimum slip angle for maximum cornering force at all times in a corner. This is not an easy task.

Total Weight

Lighter is better. For competition purposes, most classes have minimum weight rules. If there is no minimum weight rule, run as light as you can. There are two big reasons that minimum weight is important. First, the

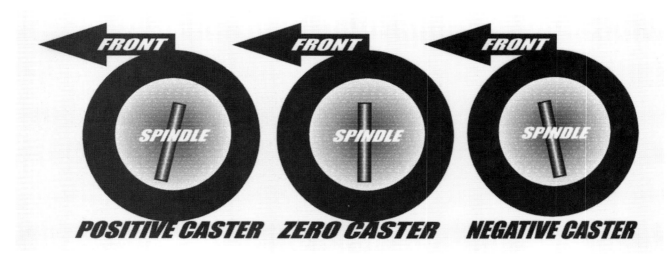

These illustrations show different caster angles.

Toe-in, toe-out, and zero toe are shown here.

engine must accelerate any extra weight along with the bare essentials. You have probably noticed that your street car does not accelerate as well with three passengers on board as it does with just you in the car. Second is the factor we looked at above: tire traction versus vertical load on the tire. The increase in traction produced by the increased vertical load is less than the required rise in tractional force necessary to keep the heavier car planted around a turn. Therefore, a heavier car cannot corner as well as a lighter one.

Weight Transfer

During cornering weight transfers from the inside to the outside, under braking from the rear to the front, and under acceleration from the front to the rear. Weight transfer hurts overall vehicle traction. In cornering situations, weight moves off the inside tires to the outside tires. This changes vertical load on all four tires. Two tires (the inside) lose vertical load while the other two gain vertical load. The inside tires lose traction while the outside tires gain traction. Sounds OK so far, but remember that the relationship between vertical load on a tire and the traction force of that tire is NOT linear. The weight coming off the inside tires causes them to lose traction faster, then the outside tires gain traction from the newfound additional vertical load. So the net total traction of the tires is reduced compared to the same situation if no weight transfer occurred. Since it is not possible to eliminate weight transfer in a corner, we at least want to minimize it so that the overall traction remains as high as possible.

Under braking, the same thing occurs but is less pronounced. Under acceleration on a rear-drive car, weight transfer actually helps accelerate the car because the drive wheels are gaining traction while the tires losing traction are not driving the car. The opposite is true for a front-drive car, which makes the elapsed times of the front-driver import drag cars all the more impressive. Even though we gain some acceleration traction from more weight transfer, if you have to turn and slow down for corners, weight transfer hurts lap times, so our goal is to minimize weight transfer as much as possible.

Following are the only four factors that affect the amount of weight transferred:

- The total weight of the vehicle: more weight means more weight transfer, all else being equal.
- The force acting on the center of gravity: more force means more weight transfer.
- The height of the center of gravity above ground: higher centers of gravity transfer more weight.
- The track width (for cornering) or the wheelbase (for acceleration and braking): narrower track width or shorter wheelbase means more weight transfer.

Effects of Weight Transfer

Let's look more closely at each of these. We have already discussed total weight. Since we want to run as light as possible, or at minimum weight, this is a constant factor that we cannot change unless we make major changes to the vehicle. The traction force of the tires determines the force acting at the center of gravity. Reducing the traction or driving below the limits of tire traction are certainly contrary to our goal of getting around the track as fast as possible; so again, this is not really a factor.

Maximum track width is always set by rules in competition or by practical considerations on street vehicles, and unless you are running at very high speeds where aerodynamic drag is a big factor, you want to run the widest track width possible. Again, this not a controllable factor. But the center of gravity, the point within the car where it, if suspended at that point, would be in perfect balance, can be altered. Maybe not much on some cars, but enough to affect performance. Simply keeping weight as low as possible in the car will lower the center of gravity, thus reducing

These two photos show body roll from the rear with stock suspension (left) versus modified suspension. (right) Reduced body roll does not reduce weight transfer, but it does decrease camber change. Stiffer antiroll bars and springs resist roll, improve response to steering inputs, and allow the handling balance (roll couple distribution) to be adjusted more closely to neutral. *Jeff Cheechov*

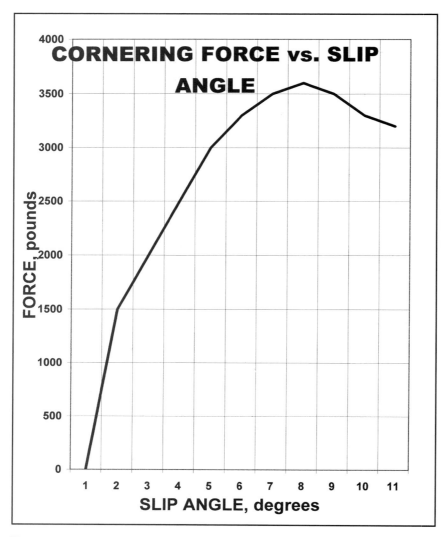

CORNERING FORCE vs. SLIP ANGLE

Tire slip angle is related to lateral acceleration and, therefore, traction. As slip angle increases, so does lateral acceleration, up to a point. Lateral acceleration levels off, then reduces as slip angle continues to increase. This graph shows that maximum cornering force occurs when all of the tires operate at 8 degrees of slip angle in a turn. Any greater or smaller slip angle means the car is not going around the corner at the maximum speed. Very high cornering force is available from 7 degrees to 9 degrees. The driver at 9 degrees is going the same speed as the driver at 7 degrees, but the driver at 9 degrees will overheat the tires sooner and cornering force will deteriorate sooner.

weight transfer. This is very important to consider when modifying the suspension and lowering a car that also lowers the center of gravity.

There are many misconceptions about weight transfer. Only the four items listed affect the amount of weight transfer. Body roll has a minimal effect and should not be considered a factor. Dive and squat are not factors. Neither is the phase of the moon. So do not be misled to believe that anything other than the four factors listed have an effect on the amount of weight transferred while cornering, braking, or accelerating.

Roll Couple Distribution

Roll couple is the total amount of roll resistance present in a car. Roll resistance is generated by the springs and antiroll bars. Stiffer springs and antiroll bars reduce body roll. Body roll is not necessarily a bad thing in itself, but it does cause some dynamics within the car that can hurt handling and overall performance. The most significant problems are increased camber change and aerodynamics. Camber change causes the tire contact patch to become loaded unequally across the tire surface, even to the point that part of the tire contact patch loses contact with the road. This requires more negative camber to counteract, which can cause the same problem under straight-line braking—part of the contact patch is not in firm contact with the road. Reducing body roll will reduce this effect. On the aero side, roll at the front allows more air under part of the car, causing aerodynamic lift and increasing aero drag. This is a big factor in competition and gets worse as speeds increase.

Body roll occurs when a car corners. Body roll is caused by weight transfer, but body roll does not cause weight transfer. Reducing body roll does not reduce weight transfer. Weight transfer in corners occurs even with zero body roll, even on a vehicle with no suspension, such as a go-cart.

Where roll couple is the total amount of resistance to body roll provided by the springs and antiroll bars at both front and rear, roll couple distribution is the amount of roll resistance at the front relative to the amount at the rear. Changing the roll couple distribution balance changes the handling balance of the car. If we increase the front roll resistance, the handling balance will change. If the car was neutral before the change, the car will now understeer. If the car understeered prior to the change, it will understeer more, and if it oversteered, it will oversteer less after the change. The opposite effect occurs at the rear, where increasing rear roll resistance will increase oversteer or reduce understeer. The roll resistance can be increased by increasing either the spring rates or the antiroll bar rates, or both. This makes roll resistance changes the key to finding a perfect steady-state handling balance.

Adjustable antiroll bars allow fine-tuning of the roll couple distribution, making setup much easier.

While body roll is not directly related to the amount of weight transfer during cornering, roll couple distribution determines where the weight is transferred, front versus rear, during cornering. Increasing front roll resistance forces more of the total weight being transferred to go to the front tires and less to the rear tires. Increasing rear roll resistance forces more of the weight being transferred to go to the rear tires. The load change on the tires, more at one end and less at the other, is what changes the handling balance. This works exactly the way you would expect based on the effects of vertical load on tire traction we discussed earlier.

Traction Circle

The traction circle is a graphic representation of tire traction used for cornering, braking, and acceleration. Tires can make traction in any direction: forward for acceleration, rearward for braking, and laterally for cornering. The rubber molecules at the tire contact patch do not know or care which direction they work in. For this reason, all of a tire's traction can be used in one direction, or part can be used for cornering and part for either braking or acceleration. Study the accompanying illustration to fully understand this principle.

The Driver

Often overlooked as a vehicle dynamics factor, the driver is actually a major factor. The driver controls when dynamic events occur based on when the driver uses one or more of the controls. And the driver determines, at least in part, how quickly dynamic events occur based on how fast and abruptly the driver uses the controls. Many drivers are too abrupt with control inputs and upset the dynamic balance of the chassis, which degrades overall vehicle performance.

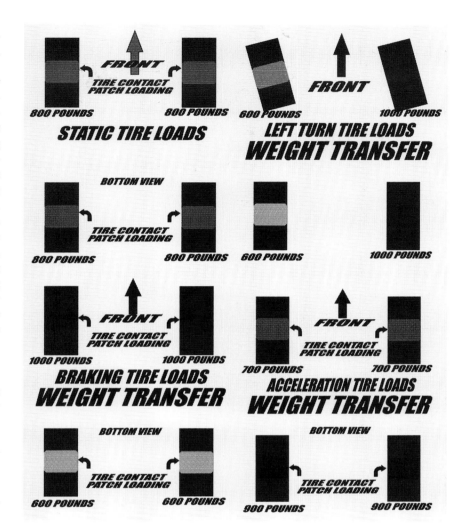

These illustrations compare weight distribution in a car at rest to the same car in a corner, during braking and acceleration. Weight moves to the outside in the corner, to the front while braking, and to the rear during acceleration.

In midcorner, the car is in steady state cornering and the handling balance should be very close to neutral with no understeer or oversteer present.

This car shows excellent midcorner balance at the limits of traction with little body roll and excellent tire contact patch compliance with the road surface. *Jeff Cheechov*

How well a car transitions while changing directions at the limits of tire traction is very important to performance. This car shows exceptional transient handling response. *Jeff Cheechov*

inputs. For cars used primarily on the street, additional factors must be considered when modifying the suspension. Ride comfort, suspension travel, ground clearance, and noise levels are factors we will consider later.

What's Possible

Street car–based racecars are limited by rules about things such as tire size and type, suspension modifications, and weight. But many stock-based racecars can achieve cornering forces in excess of 1.0-g, some in excess of 1.4-gs.

But what about on the street? What is really possible? In the project car section of this book, we have two street cars. Both are front-drive Hondas that are daily drivers and are capable of 1.0-g cornering force. To reach that level, we ran them on DOT-legal race-compound tires. These tires wear quickly due to the soft rubber compounds, but they could be used on the street. We couldn't hit the magic 1.0-g mark with ultra-high-performance road tires, but both cars got close enough to scare the average passenger silly on an interstate ramp. For all practical purposes, 0.95-g would have the same effect. That level of grip is awesome for any street-driven vehicle.

Let's put g force into perspective. A Formula One car corners in high-speed turns at 3.5-gs, an Indy Car at 2.5-gs, and a British Touring Car at about 1.5-gs. The F1 and Indy cars have enough downforce at 190 miles per hour to triple the load on the tires. That accounts for most of the traction. A British Touring Car races on slicks. They all have state-of-the-art, extremely rigid chassis structures, sophisticated suspension systems, and none of them would last 30 seconds on the streets we drive each day. So, any car that could be comfortably driven on the streets and highways of your neighborhood

The Overall Goal

If you are competing, it is important to keep in mind that the singular goal is to get around (or down) the race track as fast as possible, whether for a single lap or an entire race. For the street and highway, improving handling balance and braking performance makes your vehicle more fun to drive and improves safety. Vehicle dynamics relates ultimately to tire traction at the tire contact patch. Optimizing traction on the complete car means faster lap times, less tire wear, and safer highway driving. We can do this by manipulating the chassis components and the driver's steering, braking, and accelerator

This British Touring Car has little body roll or dive while braking and just beginning to turn into a corner. These cars have very high roll rates and springs rates, but race on smooth surfaces. They are exceptionally nimble and responsive.

Exiting a corner under full throttle acceleration, as shown here, requires good handling balance and high degrees of traction at the drive wheels, as demonstrated on this front-drive Honda Accord British Touring Car.

and bushing, must be designed for a specific application. It's not a matter of grabbing parts and bolting them on the car; an effective system must use components that are designed to work together. It doesn't matter if the car is designed for road racing, rallying, autocrossing, track days, or just street driving, the package should be designed for the type of vehicle and the activities planned for it. Here are some priorities.

Competition

- Maximum traction
- Adequate suspension travel andoptimum suspension frequencies for surface conditions
- Maximum responsiveness to driver control inputs (maximize braking, steering, cornering)
- Class rules
- Driver comfort

Performance Street Applications Only

- Adequate suspension travel
- Ground clearance
- Occupant comfort
- Overall traction
- Responsiveness to driver control inputs

and exceed 1.0-g cornering force would be quite a machine.

Just what is 1.0-g cornering force? One g is the force of gravity and equals an acceleration of 32.2 feet per second squared. Remember the science class question, What falls faster, a pound of lead or a pound of feathers? The answer is that they both fall at the same rate (with no air resistance). That rate is 1.0-g, but g forces apply to more than falling objects. Acceler-ation, deceleration, and changes in direction all create forces we can compare to the force of gravity. Going around corners at 1.0-g means that the tires are making traction equivalent to the weight of the car.

To put this into time perspective, 30 years ago, the Trans-Am Camaro campaigned by Roger Penske and driven by the legendary Mark Donahue could barely muster a two-way average of 0.90-gs on the skid pad. Today's super cars, such as the Calloway Corvette or Saleen Mustang, are not able to pull 1.0-g lateral acceleration on the skid pad. But they get close. With the right wheel, tire, and suspension modifications, many cars are capable of getting close to 1.0-g cornering force with very-high-performance

tires. Purpose-built racecars with rock-hard suspension and super-sticky, super-wide racing slicks—like Winston Cupcars—pull about 1.3 gs.

Suspension Modifications

To achieve improved handling performance, a complete system, including wheels, tires, springs, antiroll bars,

This front-drive Renault Clio racecar shows good grip accelerating from a corner, even though the inside front tire is virtually off the road surface.

This VW Improved Touring racecar is experiencing excessive understeer in midcorner due to too much front roll couple.

Dual-Purpose Vehicles (Street plus Autocross/Track Days)

All of the above are priorities, but not in the same order. The best case is to have a set of street wheels/tires and another set for track use. Coil-over suspension allows ride height to adjust easily. An adjustable antiroll bar allows fine-tuning of handling balance for the track. Urethane suspension bushings

Too little rear traction brings oversteer, which will cause a spin when extreme. *Jeff Cheechov*

allow a good compromise between ride harshness and quick responsiveness.

In all of the above cases, the system and all of its components must be matched or designed to work together to achieve the desired results. Several companies provide excellent packages to achieve any desired level of performance. An experienced tuning shop will provide the expertise needed to

create the best possible package for your needs.

Street Packages

If your goal is to improve street handling performance, you'll need a package designed for that purpose to achieve all of the desired compromises. On the handling side of the performance equation, we are attempting to improve cornering and braking performance without destroying ride quality. The aggressive nature of the wheel/tire combo should provide the necessary traction and responsiveness that a performance enthusiast is looking for, but without the suspension modifications the tire contact patches will not comply with the road surface correctly. The increased traction causes body roll to increase, and that causes even more camber change during cornering. More camber means less of the tire contact patch is firmly contacting the road surface, so traction is less than it could be. By controlling the body roll with stiffer springs and antiroll bars, camber change decreases and the tire contact patches comply with the road surface more firmly. There are trade-offs, however.

The Traction Circle

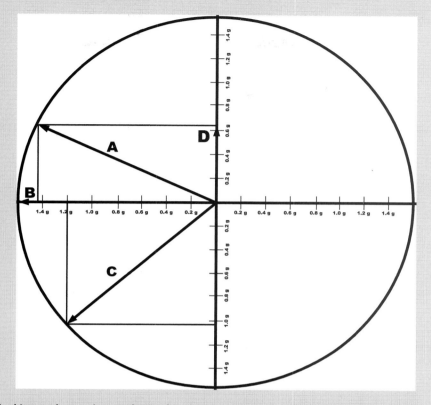

The traction circle represents the maximum traction the tires on a car are capable of generating. The radius of the circle represents maximum traction or acceleration. Acceleration can be lateral (cornering, either left or right), which is represented on the lateral axis of the circle, or longitudinal (deceleration or acceleration), which is represented on the vertical axis of the circle. The farther from the center of the circle, the greater the traction force. The circle shows the maximum traction available. The closer to the radius of the circle, the faster the car will go for a given set of circumstances. Traction is nondirectional. The traction force at given time can be a point anywhere within the radius of the circle. In other words, the traction the tires make can be used for cornering, accelerating or braking, and cornering can be combined with either acceleration or braking in varying amounts. If the driver can always use maximum traction, that driver will be faster. If the traction falls below the maximum at any time, the driver is losing time. In this diagram, arrow A shows the traction being used for both cornering to the left and acceleration. This would be the case at the exit of a turn. Arrow B shows all of the traction being used to corner to the left. Arrow C shows half of the traction being used to brake, with half used to turn left. This would be the case in midturn. Arrow D shows all traction being used to accelerate. Few cars will accelerate as quickly as they brake or corner. Acceleration is usually limited to the traction of just two tires and engine horsepower.

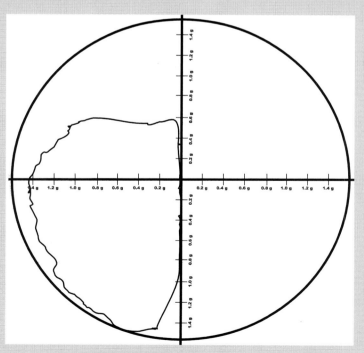

This is a good example of a real-world scenario on a traction circle diagram. The wavy line shows that tire forces are very close to the limits of traction available. The small changes in forces are due to bumps in the surface, driver use of controls, mostly small corrections, changes in track surface, and flex in the tire.

With stiffer springs and shocks, along with low-profile plus-sized tires and wheels, the ride quality is compromised. Lowering a car improves appearance and cornering, but ride quality deteriorates due to less suspension travel and stiffer components. And the reduction in ground clearance also causes problems with scraping over bumps, ruts, and driveways.

The key is finding a company that makes the best package for your application, such as those on the project cars mentioned later in the book.

Several of our project cars have achieved 1.0 g, or have come close. To get a car to corner at or near 1.0 g is all about traction and controlling that traction. The traction comes from the tires. The rubber compound and the area of the tire contact patches are the key factors. Add more rubber to the road, and the traction increases. Make the rubber softer and the traction increases, but so does tire wear. Bigger, softer tires are only part of the story. If the tire contact

patches do not stay in touch with the road surface, traction is reduced or even lost.

The suspension system must be designed to allow those sticky tires to work in a variety of road and driving conditions. For example, the springs have two jobs. First, they need to keep the car from bottoming either on the road surface or on the suspension linkages. If you lower a car, then the springs must be stiffer to control this; but that hurts ride quality if you go too far. Second, the springs must allow the tire contact patch to stay on the road surface over bumps. If a spring is too stiff for a given bump, the tire loses compliance with the road. This ruins traction and handling performance; if a spring is too soft, body roll is excessive and the tire contact patch will lean, meaning that some of the patch is not loaded and that too reduces traction. Antiroll bars must be designed to work with a given spring combination to control roll and help

keep that tire contact flat on the road surface during cornering.

Effects of Wheel, Tire, and Suspension Modifications
Changing to High-Performance Tires, Ultra-High-Performance Tires, and Wider Tires

Improves: Braking performance, acceleration performance, cornering performance (sometimes)

Problems: Accelerated tire wear, increased body roll causing more camber change and less cornering traction, increased ride harshness

Stiffer Suspension Springs

Improves: Lower ride height for better handling and looks, reduced body roll for improved tire traction, quicker response to driver steering inputs, improved handling balance if well engineered

Problems: Harsher ride, handling balance too extreme if poorly engineered, cut or poorly engineered springs

The inside car in this photo has a neutral handling balance, while the outside car is understeering. Note the angles of the front wheels of the two cars.

can allow suspension or chassis to bottom out leading to potential damage or crashes

Stiffer Suspension Antiroll Bars

Improves: Reduced body roll for improved tire traction, quicker response to driver steering inputs, improved handling balance if well engineered

Problems: Slightly harsher ride, handling balance too extreme if poorly engineered

Stiffer Suspension Bushings

Improves: Quicker response to driver steering inputs, less compliance in suspension for improved tire wear and handling

Problems: Harsher ride, sometimes noisier

Stiffer Shock Absorber Rates

Improves: Quicker response to driver steering inputs, better feel of steering, improved handling during cornering, braking, and acceleration transitions when valving is correct for application

Problems: Harsher ride, handling deterioration if incorrectly valved for application

Competition Packages

A competition package is even easier to create in some respects than a street package. There are fewer compromises because ride quality is not an issue. Everything must be perfect, however. Total tire traction is the most significant goal. Suspension alignment, cross-weight (see chapter 14), roll couple distribution, suspension frequencies, shock rates, and responsiveness must all be perfect to achieve maximum total traction.

In all cases, a well-designed system made from quality materials will ensure that you realize your goals. Consult with manufacturers or dealers. Web sites and catalogs provide excellent information, and many companies

The inside rear tire is off the racing surface in this photo. This indicates considerable rear roll couple distribution, which on a front-drive car such as this Ford Fiesta, is needed to ensure the optimum handling balance.

Here the lead car is accelerating and the following car is still under braking. In both cases, the cars are also turning. Note the inside rear tire of the trailing car and the inside front tire of the car in front. Both are unloaded. This shows a good balance of roll couple distribution on these cars, and it also depicts the effects of weight transfer while turning and braking versus turning and cornering.

have trained sales staffs to help you with specific applications.

Suspension Alignment

After making any suspension modifications (as opposed to just wheel and tire changes), have the alignment checked. In most cases, realignment will be required. For street, use factory settings for toe, camber, and caster. For competition, use the component manufacturer's specs, or refer to the alignment chapter in this book.

Chapter Three
Shocks and Springs

Shock absorbers play a critical role in handling performance both on the highway and the racetrack.

Shocks don't actually absorb shocks, but rather they dampen vibrations. Shocks are often called dampers for that reason. The shock is designed to control movements of the suspension, working in conjunction with the springs. The springs actually absorb shocks over bumps and control body roll. The shocks control the oscillations of the springs, determining how fast the spring moves up and down. Stiffer shock rates slow spring movements, while a softer shock rate allows the spring to move faster. A shock is way too soft if it allows the springs to oscillate, or bounce, more than one full cycle. You've probably driven, or seen, a car with worn shocks bouncing down the road after hitting a bump. A shock is way too stiff if the shock limits spring travel.

Bumps

If the shock is too stiff, a bump can throw the tire contact patch right off the track surface, or at least reduce the load on that tire significantly. This affects handling balance and moves weight around the chassis, making the car feel unpredictable. The loss of traction is considerable and the car is very hard for the driver to read. Over bumps, the car feels like it skates.

A shock dampens vibrations by creating friction. Racing shocks all use hydraulic fluid in a tube with a piston. The piston pushes the fluid through a series of valves and bleeds, controlling the "rate" of the shock. The valves and bleed can be varied to change the rate. Different valves and bleeds are used for rebound and compression and different valves are used for different shaft speeds. The valves for either rebound or compression at various shaft speeds can be changed together or independently to vary the shock's response over bumps or during body roll and pitch (falling or rising off the front or rear end) under braking and acceleration.

In general terms, different shaft speeds come into play for different jobs. Roll and pitch involve slow shaft speeds. The valving for slow shaft speed has the greatest effect on transitional handling, and when a shock is adjustable, it is usually the low-speed valving that can be altered. High shaft speeds come into play over bumps and ruts and affect the tire contact patch. Medium shaft speeds have an influence over both handling and bumps.

There are several types of shock designs, but all have the same effect on the chassis. Some shocks are gas charged and some are not. The differences are mostly in design, performance as heat builds up, wear, reliability, and rebuilding potential.

Compression and Rebound Damping

Bump, or compression, occurs when the shock shaft is being moved into the body. This occurs on the front of a bump, the back of a rut, the right side when turning left, the left side when exiting a left turn, the front under braking, and the rear under acceleration.

Rebound, or extension, occurs when the shaft is being pulled from the body. This occurs on the backside of a bump, the front of a rut, the left side shocks in a left turn, the right side shocks exiting a left turn, the front under acceleration, and the rear under braking.

Shaft Speeds

Shocks work mostly within a range of about 3 inches per second to

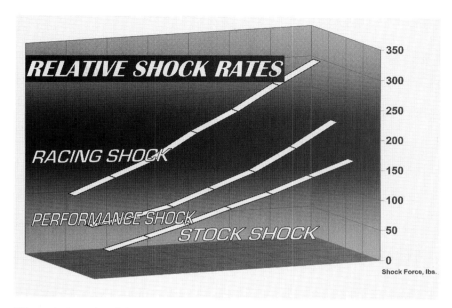

This graph shows the relative stiffness of shock absorbers used in a variety of applications.

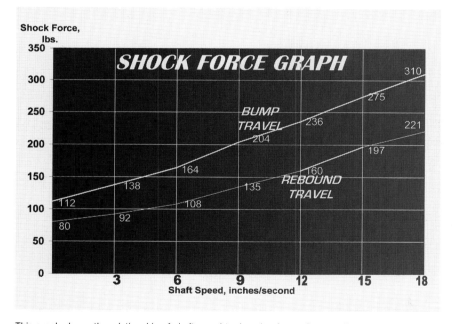

This graph shows the relationship of shaft speed to damping force of a nonadjustable shock in both bump and rebound travel.

about 20 inches per second. The lower speeds come into play during weight transfer when the body is rolling or pitching. The higher speeds come into play over bumps and ruts. A shock manufacturer can alter low-, medium-, and high-speed valving to control what the shock does in different situations. Low- and medium-speed valving are used to control how the shock influences handling.

How Shocks Affect Weight Transfer

There are four components to weight transfer.

• *How much weight is transferred:*
This is controlled by the weight of

The shock on top is in full rebound or extension. The shock in the middle is at full compression or bump, while the one on the bottom is at standard ride height.

the car, the track width/wheelbase, the center of gravity height, and the cornering force.

- *Where weight is transferred:* This is controlled by the spring rates acting at the tire contact patch, the antiroll bar rates, and some lateral locating bars on rear suspensions.
- *When weight is transferred:* This is controlled when the driver uses the controls: the steering, brakes, and accelerator.
- *How fast weight is transferred:* This controlled by the shock rates and by how fast the driver uses the controls.

How Shocks Affect Handling

The low- and medium-speed valving of the shock controls how fast weight is transferred. This affects the load on a tire and can change the handling balance while weight is being transferred. Once all weight has been transferred, the shock no longer influences handling. Since weight is almost always being transferred, the shocks are almost always affecting handling balance.

In general, rebound damping controls how fast weight leaves a tire while bump damping controls how fast weight goes onto a tire. Stiffer valving

causes a shock to react more quickly; softer valving slows the reaction of the shock. Stiffer valving gets the load to change more quickly. Stiffer rebound valving gets the load off a tire more quickly and onto an opposite tire faster. Stiffer bump valving gets the load onto that tire faster. If all the valving, both bump and rebound at all four corners, changes equally, there is no effect on handling balance. If only

bump or rebound is changed, then there is an effect. If only one end or one corner is changed, there is also an effect. We will look more closely at this in a later chapter.

How the Driver Affects the Shocks

Very fast steering-wheel movements cause the body to roll faster and change the shaft speed of the shocks. This increases the rate of the shock and

Shocks affect transient handling response. In general, higher valving forces result in quicker chassis response to driver control inputs. *Jeff Cheechov*

Shocks will not affect the amount of body roll or weight transfer, but have a major influence on how quickly roll and weight transfer take place. *Jeff Donker*

affects handling by changing the rate of weight transfer. This can be compounded by the fact that the driver is most often using more than one control at a time. How fast the driver turns the steering wheel and how fast the driver pushes on the brake pedal have a big impact on the handling going into a corner. For this reason that the driver must be really smooth when using the controls. Abrupt steering or pedal applications can affect the handling in a negative way, and it can be very tough to tune the chassis to overcome this.

Split Valve and Adjustable Shocks

Split valve shocks have different valving in the bump and rebound phases, which allows precise chassis tuning for certain track situations. For example, "tie down" shocks, which rebound slowly, might be used on the left rear to slow weight transfer to the right rear; "easy up" shocks, which rebound quickly, can be used up front to allow for quick weight transfer to the rear for better traction accelerating out of corners. Adjustable shocks allow the user to vary rebound rate only or both bump and rebound rates (double adjustable). Shock absorbers

are typically tuned while still on the car. For the most part, tuning the shocks is considered a fine-tuning adjustment and is addressed once the chassis is set up and tuned.

Travel

Shock travel—the total distance the shock moves in and out—is very important. The more travel, the better

the shock can do its job. Lowering a car without swapping out the stock shocks reduces or even eliminates compression travel. Reduced compression travel, in turn, can lead to shock or strut damage or handling problems serious enough to cause a loss of control. If you lower your car, you should include shocks as part of a coordinated suspension package to provide adequate suspension travel and improved performance.

For racing, shocks should be mounted as close to the ball joint on a front lower control arm as possible, and as close to the hub on the rear axle; but do not compromise clearance with components, and on the front, check clearance during full steering travel.

Bottoming Out

If a shock bottoms out or reaches full extension under load, damage can occur. Bump stops on the shaft of the shocks reduce this, and some shock or strut manufacturers use rebound travel limiters to keep the shock from reaching full extension. Full extension is then usually less of a problem.

Cooling

Shocks dampen by using friction, which causes heat. Heat buildup can

Shocks that are too stiff for an application or driver experience can create a car that responds too abruptly during transitions. This can cause a handling problem, understeer or oversteer, while the car is perfectly balanced during steady state cornering.

Shocks also influence weight transfer during acceleration and braking. This is especially important when entering a turn under braking or exiting with acceleration. *Jeff Donker*

Dyno Testing Shocks

Dyno testing a shock gives the owner exact data on the bump and rebound rates at several shaft speeds. Once a workable combination is found, that combination can be repeated if and when a shock needs to be rebuilt or replaced. You can also tell if a shock is worn, and how much by testing on a shock dyno.

Rebuilding Shocks

Some shocks can be easily rebuilt, and it's usually much cheaper to do so than to buy a new one. In general, steel body shocks from most manufacturers cannot be rebuilt, while many aluminum body shocks can. Check with your dealer or shock manufacturer.

Springs

The heart of a suspension system is the springs. Springs perform five critical jobs. First, they keep the chassis and suspension from bottoming out over bumps. Second, they control the tires over bumps. Third, they control body roll during cornering, chassis squat during acceleration, and chassis dive under braking. Fourth, the springs determine how the load on the tires shifts during braking, cornering, and acceleration. This makes them a pivotal component in establishing the neutral

affect the rate of the shock, always softening it. Dissipating heat always helps shock performance. Bumpy tracks create more heat than do smooth tracks. It is best not to cover shocks and even to duct cool air to the shocks. Aluminum shocks dissipate heat faster than steel bodies. For coil-overs, threaded body shocks cool better than smooth body shocks with threaded spring perches over the body for the coil-over adjusters.

Analyzing Shocks

Shocks should be checked regularly for binds and pitting in the shafts. It is a good idea to check for dead spots by extending the shock fully and putting a sudden load on the shock by hand. Do the same with the shock fully compressed and pull out the shaft abruptly. A dead spot will be obvious, and that shock needs to rebuilt or replaced.

Coil-over shocks like these Progress Competition shocks are ideal for competition since they allow easy ride height adjustments for fine-tuning cross-weights and handling balance. *Progress Group*

handling balance of the car. And finally, the springs are the major factor in establishing the ride height (ground clearance) of the chassis. The series of compromises needed to create the ideal setup for a given car and performance application require experience, sound engineering, and testing.

Sport springs should lower the car, which also lowers the center of gravity and improves handling performance. But if the springs are not stiff enough at the lower ground clearance, the chassis or suspension will bottom, causing damage to the chassis or suspension. If the springs are too stiff, the ride is horrible and tire contact patch control over bumps deteriorates. For a competition situation, ride comfort is not an issue, but controlling the tire contact patch over bumps is a major concern. Bumpy surfaces require softer springs than smooth surfaces. This compromise is critical.

On the highway, a good set of sport springs from a reputable manufacturer, designed and tested for aggressive street applications, will offer a good compromise between performance and an acceptable ride. Springs designed for racing applications, whether stock replacement springs or coil-over racing springs, will prove too stiff for either comfort or tire control over bumps, so that is not the best way to go. Often ride height is a concern with more aggressive springs. Sticking with a package designed for highway use is the best course to follow.

Chassis Tuning with Springs for Competition

Last month, you won your class at the club event. During registration for this event, one of your fellow racers asks what springs you run. You tell him. He changes his springs to what you run. In practice, his car pushes right off the course. The understeer was extreme and your fellow racer, unscathed but embarrassed and mad, thinks you lied to him about your spring rates. You didn't. He just has a

For street and occasional motorsports use, coil-overs, like these H & R units on an Audi, allow ride height adjustments for more or less ground clearance depending on needs. The H & R coil-overs allow low ride heights for autocrossing or track days, moderate ride heights for street use, and tall ride heights for off-road and winter snow conditions. They also use hard rubber bushings for less vibration and noise, a plus for use on a daily driver.

different make of car than you and the wheel rates and suspension frequencies are different on his car, so the information he got from you was not only useless, but when used, caused him to fall off the track.

This is only one of the pitfalls when tuning the chassis with springs. Tuning handling balance (push versus loose) with springs is a common practice in racing, and rightfully so. Springs exercise a large influence on handling balance. But handling balance is not the only job the springs must accomplish. In fact, it is not even the most important job.

The primary job of the springs in a racing application is to keep the tire contact patch loaded and on the racing surface over bumps and ruts. If a spring is too soft, it will oscillate or bounce, causing an uneven vertical load on the tire. If a spring is too stiff, the tire will unload too much over bumps, even losing contact with the racing surface. As we've seen, reducing load on a tire reduces traction, so the spring has a very important job. The range of

spring rates that will control the tire contact patch over bumps is fairly large. Within that range, you can use the springs to fine-tune handling balance. Changes in spring rate as small as 2 percent will affect roll couple enough to make a difference. If a larger change is necessary to achieve the desired handling balance, the antiroll bar should be used.

The secondary job of the spring is to help control the oversteer/understeer (loose/push) handling balance of the chassis. The springs work with antiroll bars to do this as well as control the degree of body roll while cornering. The springs and bars work together to control where transferred weight goes, front versus rear. The amount of weight transferred at the front versus the rear changes vertical loading on the tires, which changes traction. When the front springs (or antiroll bar) are stiffened while the rears remain the same, more weight transfer occurs at the front. The outcome is that with the front stiffness increased versus the rear, the front has relatively

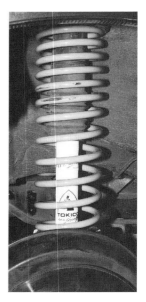

The Tokico Illumina shock is not a coil-over but has as an external adjustment for rebound damping. This allows for a more comfortable ride on the softest setting, and much more responsive handling on the stiffer settings. Additionally, these adjustments allow fine-tuning the front or rear rebound rates to adjust transient handling balance.

less traction while the rear has more, so the car will tend toward the understeer direction of handling balance.

Wheel Rates

In the scenario above, one driver wanted to know the spring rates of the last event's winner. Knowing the spring rates on another car is, frankly, useless information. On the other hand, knowing the wheel rates can be very useful data, up to a point.

The wheel rate of a spring is the actual rate of the spring acting at the center of the tire contact patch. The wheel rate is nothing more than the spring multiplied by leverage factors. Unless a spring is mounted at the centerline of the wheel, or you have on open-wheel car with bellcranks and pushrod suspension linkages, the wheel rate of a spring is always less than the actual spring rate.

To determine the wheel rate of a spring, we must first know the motion ratio of the suspension linkage to which the spring mounts and which moves the spring during suspension travel. Most cars have the spring mounted to the chassis at the top and

to either the rear axle housing or the lower control arm at the front. As an example, let's take a lower control arm that measures 16 inches from the center of the inner pivot to the center of the outer ball joint. If the spring is mounted to the lower control arm so that the exact centerline of the spring is 8 inches from the inner pivot center, then we can find the motion ratio by dividing the length of the control arm (16 inches) by the distance from the spring centerline to the inner pivot center (8 inches). In our example, the motion ratio is .5 inches.

The motion ratio actually affects the spring rate in two ways. First is the effect of leverage, like a teeter-totter or pry bar. In our example, the leverage on the spring is exactly one-half, so now our spring rate is effectively 50 percent of what it would be if it were at the centerline of the wheel. Second is the issue of travel, since we calculate springs in pounds per inch. When the wheel moves up (or down) by 1 inch, the spring travels less. In our example, since the spring is 50 percent of the distance from the inner pivot to the ball joint center, then the spring

will travel only 50 percent as much as the wheel. In our example, if we started with a 1,000-pound-per-inch spring rate, the rate of that spring acting at the wheel would be 1,000 pounds times .5 (the leverage factor portion of the motion ratio). That result would then be multiplied by .5 (the travel factor of the motion ratio). Thus the wheel rate of our 1,000-pound spring equals 1,000 times .5 times .5, or 1,000 times .5 squared. This becomes 1,000 times .25, which equals the wheel rate of the spring acting at the center of the tire contact patch. In this example, that force—the wheel rate—is only 250 pounds per inch of travel. The wheel rate equals 250 pounds per inch.

There are two additional factors that affect the wheel rate, though they are minor in most cases. The first is the mounting angle of the spring from vertical. The correction factor for the mounting angle of the spring is the sine of the angle times the spring rate or the wheel rate. In our example, we already have a wheel rate from the motion ratio, so the solution is found by multiplying the cosine of the angle times

250. Let's say the angle is 7 degrees, not very large. The cosine of 7 degrees is .993, so the new, improved wheel rate is 250 times .993, or 248 pounds. This is nearly insignificant in the big picture. Angles of 10 degrees or less have very small effects on the wheel rate and can be ignored. More than 10 degrees and the effect becomes significant. At 30 degrees, for example, the cosine is .867, so the wheel rate takes a bigger hit, dropping from 250 pounds to 217 pounds.

The final variable is so complex and difficult to change that its solution is beyond the scope of this book. Fortunately, it is seldom a significant problem. This particular motion ratio is measured from the outer ball joint of the lower control arm to the instant center of the suspension. For reference, the instant center is the point where the line extending the upper control arm meets the line extending from the lower

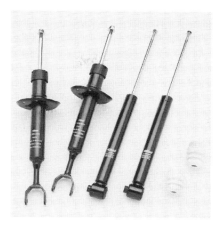

A sport shock absorber package like this one from Eibach allows improved performance for the street without significant loss in ride quality. *Eibach*

control arm. For most cars, the arm length from the ball joint to instant center is several feet. This motion ratio is found by dividing the length of the spring-centerline-to-instant-center distance by the ball-joint-to-instant-center

distance (the length of the virtual swing arm). This is usually a very large number, very close to one, so the effect is very small—unless the virtual swing arm is short.

The instant center changes length as well as moving vertically during body roll, so this effect can change as body roll changes, which means that the wheel rate can change during body roll as well. For a long virtual swingarm, say 5 feet or 60 inches, using our prior example, the distance of the spring center to the instant center is 52 inches, so the correction factor is 0.867 (52/60), which further reduces the wheel rate from 250 pounds to 217 pounds. This is a significant number.

If handling is abruptly changing in midturn and you have ruled out any type of bind, it could be extreme lateral instant center movement during body roll. If the instant center moves inward by 48 inches at the maximum

Springs play a major role in improved handling and provide a racy look. *James Brown*

The most common replacement spring is a sport spring like this installation on a front strut suspension.

of body roll, then the front spring will effectively become softer, causing a possible loose condition as body roll increases. With the instant center now at 12 inches from the ball joint, and the center of the spring only 4 inches from the instant center, the correction factor is 0.33. The wheel rate that was 217 pounds is now only 83 pounds. A big change and a potential big problem as well! This can be the core of handling problems that are very difficult to figure out. A change in suspension geometry is the real cure and for that you should secure professional assistance.

Solid axles are a little more complex. Over two wheel bumps, both springs are compressed equally, so the motion ratio is one. The spring rate equals the wheel rate. Both springs move some over a one-wheel bump. The wheel hitting the bump moves the most while the other wheel moves some, but both springs compress and influence tire contact patch control over bumps. If each spring is mounted the same distance from the tire centerline, and the spring rates are the same, then the motion ratio is still one, but only acting on the springs encountering the bump. The reason for this is that the pivot point for the axle is the tire not hitting the bump. Both springs compress and the total movement is always equal to the vertical travel of the tire hitting the bump.

Here's an example: Let's say the track width is 60 inches and the springs are separated by 30 inches, each being 15 inches inboard of the tire centerline. If the tire hitting the bump travels up 1 inch, and the other tire does not move vertically, the spring closest to the bump will move .75 inches, and the other spring will

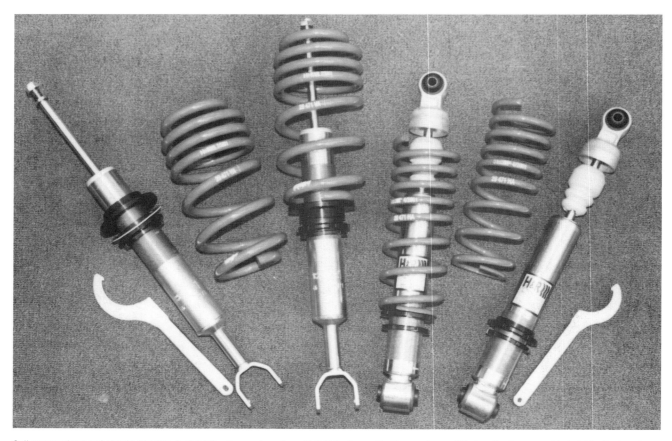

Coil-over springs and shocks like this Audi A4 Quattro package from H & R Springs offer the most versatility by allowing easy ride height adjustments.

Sport Springs from the Progress Group, like these front and rear examples for a Honda Accord, offer an excellent compromise between performance, looks, and ride quality.

move .25 inches. The total movement is 1 inch. With equal spring rates, the effective wheel rate is the rate of one spring. But if the springs are different, or the mounting points left to right are not equidistant from the tire centerline, this will be different, although the trend is the same. If nothing else, symmetrical cars are easier to figure out.

The wheel rate is important. Naturally, it is best if the wheel rate is closer to the actual spring rate. This mostly reduces the size of the spring needed to achieve a given wheel rate. For this reason, coil-over springs work better. Because the springs are smaller in diameter, the spring centerline can be mounted closer to the ball joint center, so the motion ratio is higher and smaller; lighter springs can be used to achieve the same wheel rate.

These Eibach Sport springs are progressive, which means that the rate increases as the spring is compressed. *Eibach Springs*

The threaded spring perch allows ride height adjustment on this Progress coil-over. Adjustable ride heights allow for a variety of conditions from daily driving to competition.

Suspension Frequencies

Now that we have determined how motion ratios affect wheel rates, and that springs can be used for tuning handling balance within a narrow range of spring rates, let's look at the best, most scientific method of determining how stiff a spring should be for the bumpiness of a track. The general rule of thumb is that the bumpier the track surface, the softer the spring rate required. But how soft is too soft, or not soft enough? Certainly testing, driver input, observation, and lap times are good indicators, but these take time, money, and experience. The easiest way, once you have overcome that math phobia, is to use suspension frequencies.

A frequency, as the word implies, is how often an event occurs. Springs, as we know from experience, don't just stop once they've been extended, or compressed, and then released. They oscillate, moving one way and then the other at a particular rate, or frequency. For springs, we measure this frequency in cycles per second, or CPS. One cycle per second for a spring means that the springs will compress fully, extend beyond normal free height, and compress back to static loaded height one time per second. One CPS is actually the low end of the range of frequencies for a suspension spring, with 3 CPS being toward the high-end.

Any time a suspension spring encounters a disturbance in the road surface, the spring will compress or extend. It will continue to oscillate at its natural frequency until friction reduces

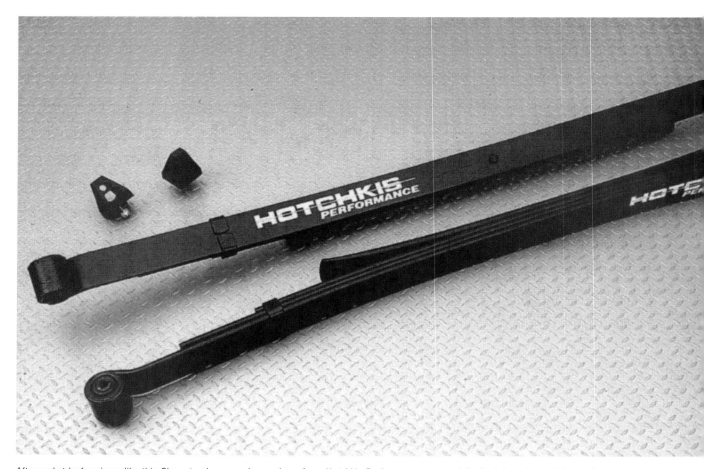

Aftermarket leaf springs, like this Chevy truck rear spring package from Hotchkis Performance, are used for both lowering and improving performance. *Hotchkis Tuning*

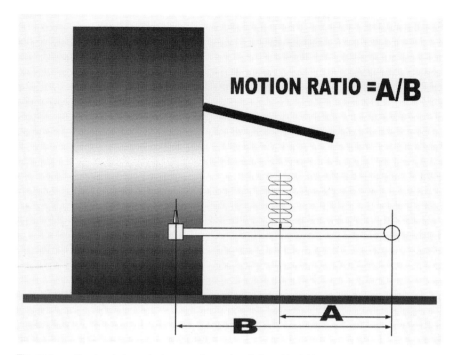

The motion ratio of an independent suspension system is found by taking exact measurements of the lower control arm from the inner pivot centerline to the outer ball joint centerline and from the inner pivot centerline to the spring centerline. The motion ratio is found by dividing the measurement from the spring centerline to the inner pivot centerline (A) by the inner pivot centerline to the ball joint centerline measurement (B).

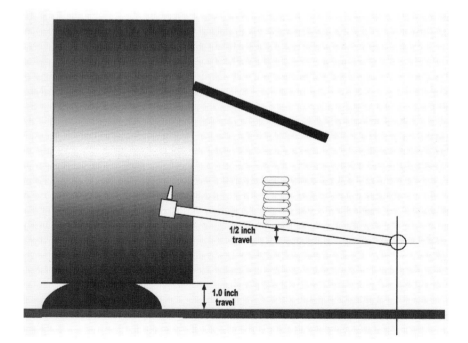

The reason the motion ratio is squared to determine wheel rates is shown here. Not only does the spring have less leverage because it is mounted inboard of the outer ball joint centerline, but its vertical movement is also less. In the example, the spring centerline to the inner pivot centerline is exactly half of the length of the ball joint centerline to the inner pivot. The motion ratio is 0.50 inches, and because of the double effect, the motion ratio is squared to determine the actual wheel rate.

or stops the movement or another disturbance disrupts the motion. On vehicles, we use shock absorbers to control and stop these oscillations. The frequency at which the spring will naturally bounce is closely related to the severity of the bumps it encounters. Very small bumps produce small amplitudes or vertical displacement of the suspension. In fact, if we were to encounter no bumps at all we could have a rigid suspension (or no suspension) and an infinitely high suspension frequency.

Going to the other extreme, on a very bumpy track, the amplitudes, or vertical wheel movements, are very big. We need very low frequencies to allow the tire contact patch to stay in touch with the racing surface. Higher frequencies will cause the tire to skate, even bounce, over the racing surface, and a tire with little or no vertical load doesn't provide much in the way of traction, let alone confidence-inspiring performance.

To find the proper spring rate for your car and conditions, start by looking at the diagram on the next page. There you will find a variety of suspension frequencies correlated with track surface smoothness conditions. They range from the ultrasmooth asphalt track with a frequency of 3.2 CPS down to the very bumpy dirt road found on rally stages at 1.2 CPS. Most tracks are in the middle, and the optimum suspension frequency for autocrossing or road racing on a slightly bumpy course will be about 1.9 to 2.2 CPS.

These frequencies are for the stiffer end of the car. The front should be a different frequency than the rear. If they are the same, at a given road speed over certain types of bumps, they can set up an oscillation between the front and rear, creating a bucking motion that is neither comfortable nor conducive to good traction or handling balance. You may have experienced this with a stiffly sprung car or when towing on an interstate.

| SMOOTH SURFACE SUSPENSION FREQUENCY = 3.2 CYCLES PER SECOND | MODERATELY BUMPY SURFACE SUSPENSION FREQUENCY = 2.2 CYCLES PER SECOND | VERY BUMPY SURFACE SUSPENSION FREQUENCY = 1.2 CYCLES PER SECOND |

Suspension frequencies are used to determine ideal wheel rates, and then springs rates, based on the surface smoothness. Smoother surfaces can tolerate higher frequencies, which require higher wheel rates and therefore higher spring rates.

Calculating Suspension Frequencies

Here is the formula for calculating suspension frequencies:

FREQUENCY = 3.13 x $\sqrt{\text{wheel rate/sprung weight}}$
(where wheel rate is in pounds per inch, sprung weight is in pounds, frequency is in cycles per second
3.13 is a constant)

EXAMPLE:
Frequency = 3.13 x $\sqrt{300/800}$

Frequency = 3.13 x $\sqrt{0.375}$

Frequency = 3.13 x 0.612372

Frequency = 1.92 CPS

The formula for wheel rate is:

Wheel rate = sprung rate x motion ratio^2
(where wheel rate is in pounds per inch, spring rate is in pounds per inch)

Example:
Wheel rate = 1,000 x 0.50^2
Wheel rate = 1,000 x 0.25
Wheel rate = 250 pounds per inch

The reason high-end racecars like this British Touring Car can run such high-suspension frequencies is the fact that the tracks are very smooth with minimal bumps.

The separation between front and rear suspension frequencies should be about 10 percent. What seems to work best is for the higher frequency to be at the drive wheels. This allows the car to run with either a smaller antiroll bar, or none at all on the drive wheel end of the vehicle. Since antiroll bars try to lift the inside tire off the ground in a corner, a stiffer bar can hurt traction exiting corners. The stiffer springs at the drive end help control body roll without resorting to a stiffer bar.

There are two primary factors affecting the spring frequency. First is the weight resting on the spring, or the sprung weight. (The sprung weight is the corner weight less the weight of items not suspended by the spring, such as wheels, tires, brakes, hubs, and half the weight of the shocks and springs.) The frequency goes down as the sprung weight goes up for a given wheel rate. The second factor is the wheel rate. If you increase the wheel rate, the frequency

gets higher. See the sidebar for details concerning frequency calculations.

The bottom line is that you must find the best compromise possible for your car, track conditions, and driving style. Tuning with springs and using suspension frequencies as a tool will help. Let good judgment, common sense, and lap times be the final factors in determining the best setup for your circumstances.

Chapter Four
Antiroll Bars, Bushings, Camber Adjusters, and Chassis Braces

Antiroll bars are an almost magical invention. They provide an excellent means for adjusting roll couple distribution (handling balance). They also control body roll, thus reducing camber change. This allows the tire contact patch to stay flatter on the road surface during cornering at the traction limit. By doing these two important jobs,

antiroll bars allow the spring rates to do their job of keeping the tire contact patches on the road surface over bumps. The front and rear antiroll bars are an excellent way to tune handling balance without affecting ride quality.

Antiroll bars attach to the chassis in bushing mounts. These mounts allow the bar to rotate but hold it firmly

in place relative to the chassis. The ends of the antiroll bar have arms that attach to the suspension with links that allow the free movement of the arms with the suspension. The arms are most often part of the bar, which is bent at or near a 90-degree angle to the chassis. Multiple bends are often used for clearance. Some antiroll bars have

Antiroll bars are critical for improved handling. Not only do they limit body roll–induced camber change, but they offer a quick and reliable means to adjust roll couple distribution and handling balance.

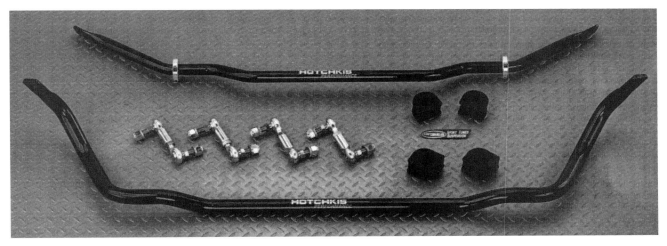

This antiroll bar package from Hotchkis Performance for a C5 Corvette is typical of the kits available. *Hotchkis Tuning*

detachable arms with splines fitting on splines on the bar itself.

When the bar is twisted, it acts like a spring, or torsion bar, providing resistance to the twisting motion. A larger-diameter bar resists twisting more, and a longer arm on the bar resists twisting less. When a vehicle turns into a corner, weight transfer causes the body to roll. Springs resist body roll, but not enough to control camber change in a high-performance or motorsports application.

The antiroll bar adds resistance to body roll, helping to control camber change as well as providing a means of tuning roll couple distribution. As the body begins to roll, the outside suspension moves into bump travel and the inside suspension moves into rebound travel. This causes the bar to twist, providing resistance to roll. This resistance is not immediate, however.

Compliance in the bushings and end links slows the twisting motion. Solid bushings and rod end–style links reduce compliance the most. Polyurethane bushings offer excellent resistance to compliance, and are good in most motorsports applications and a good compromise for the street. They offer good responsiveness without too much ride harshness and lower levels of noise and vibration. Rubber bushings have the highest degree of compliance and

are not suitable for high-performance and motorsports applications.

The downside of antiroll bars is the connection between left-side and right-side suspensions. Independent suspension is no longer truly independent with an antiroll bar. Over two-wheel bumps, the antiroll bar has no effect, but over single-wheel bumps, the bar twists, acting like a spring and adding its rate to the wheel rate of the spring. This increases the frequency of the suspension at that corner and hurts the ability of the suspension to keep the tire contact patch firmly on the road.

Types of Antiroll Bars

Antiroll bars can be made of solid bar stock or tubing, bent into the proper shape with arms at approximately right angles to the chassis-mounted section of the bar. Some racing bars are made of solid or tubular straight sections splined on the end. Arms, usually made of aluminum and also splined, provide the leverage to twist the bar.

How Antiroll Bars Influence Handling

Earlier, we discussed roll couple distribution, which is the combined resistance to body roll provided by the springs and antiroll bars at the front versus the rear. Even though antiroll

bars distribute transferred weight differently than springs, the effect is the same. If you stiffen the front antiroll bar, the understeer is increased (or oversteer decreased). If you stiffen the rear antiroll bar, the oversteer is increased (or understeer decreased). Softening a bar has the opposite effect.

If a car oversteers during steady state cornering, a softer rear antiroll bar or a stiffer front antiroll bar should help reduce or eliminate the condition. Which bar to change depends on several factors covered in the tuning section of this book.

This front bar for a VW Golf is from Autotech Sport Tuning. *Autotech Sport Tuning*

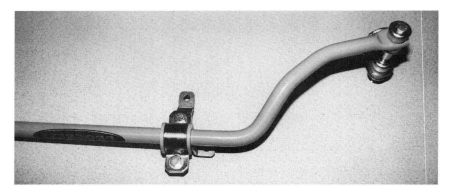

This Progress antiroll bar uses polyurethane bushings for mounting and on the adjustable end links.

This stock antiroll bar was made adjustable by adding a plate with alternate mounting holes. This part is under extreme loads and the welding should only be done by a certified welder to ensure a strong, safe mount.

The detail of an antiroll bar end link is seen here.

There are situations where increasing the stiffness of an antiroll bar will have the opposite effect. Most stock vehicles have excessive understeer because it is easier to control and provides more stability for the average driver than a vehicle that oversteers. A big part of this comes from excessive body roll, which induces too much camber change, and a good portion of the front tire contact patches loses contact with the road.

In this instance, adding a stiffer front antiroll bar, which would typically increase the extreme understeer, actual-ly reduces the understeer by reducing the body roll–induced camber change. The front tires now stay in better contact with the road surface, creating more traction and reducing understeer. This is an old trick in SCCA autocrossing in stock classes where the few modifications permitted include changing the front antiroll bar.

On a front-drive car with a front weight in excess of 59 percent, the rear bar will be quite stiff. For competition, the bar will be stiff enough to lift the inside rear tire contact patch off the ground slightly in a corner at the limits of traction. For the highway, the bar should be softer for improved stability.

Antiroll Bar Preload

Most stock antiroll bars use end links with no vertical adjustment. Most aftermarket antiroll kits use adjustable end links to eliminate antiroll bar pre-load. Preload means the bar has a twist in it while stationary.

Preload on an antiroll bar is undesirable because at some point during body roll, a preloaded bar will unload momentarily. This will happen in only one direction, depending on which way the bar is preloaded. For street driving, when the limits of tire traction are never reached in cornering, you would never notice the preload. In a competition situation at the corner limits of tire traction, the moment the bar unloads, the handling balance will abruptly change. Then, as body roll

These photos show two views of an adjustable rear antiroll bar on a VW Golf. This setup allows quick, easy handling balance adjustments by stiffening the bar (shorter lever arm) to reduce understeer.

continues, the bar will again be loaded and again the balance will change. This is both slow and unpleasant. It is very hard to drive smoothly with a pre-loaded bar, at least cornering in one direction.

Preload is eliminated by adjusting the end links so that the antiroll bar is free. This should be done at standard ride height with the driver in place. Disconnect one end link and adjust its length (longer or shorter) until it can easily be reattached without twisting the antiroll bar.

Antiroll Bar Rates

Four factors determine the rate of an antiroll bar: the diameter of the bar along its active length, the length of the antiroll bar arms, the active length of the antiroll bar, and the modulus of elasticity (strength) of the bar material. Stiffness increases at a rate of four times the increases to the bar's diameter, thus doubling the bar diameter makes the bar eight times stiffer. The active length of the roll bar and the length of the arms operate in linear fashion, with shorter length increasing stiffness and longer length reducing it in both cases. The modulus of the material, which is nearly always

high-tensile-strength steel, is considered a constant.

Because of multiple bends in a stock replacement antiroll bar, it is difficult to calculate the rates. Most manufacturers calculate rates then check the actual rate of the bar mechanically. Adjustable antiroll bars have multiple mounts on the arms to

change the arm length and therefore the bar rate.

Antiroll Bar Motion Ratios

Just like springs, antiroll bars have motion ratios. The closer the antiroll bar link is mounted to the centerline of the ball joint, the higher the motion ratio. If the ball joint on the control

A variety of chassis and suspension components are available to improve handling and performance. Bushings, strut braces, camber plates, and other items are made for a variety of applications. *James Brown*

These bushings are made with an eccentric and a hex-adjusting end so that camber or caster can be adjusted.

Adjustable Antiroll Bars

As we have said, the most convenient way to adjust roll couple distribution is by changing antiroll bar rates. And the easiest way to accomplish that is with an adjustable antiroll bar. Study the photos of adjustable antiroll bars to see how they work. To determine which adjustments to make to the bar, refer to the section on how antiroll bars affect handling, which appeared earlier in this chapter.

A wide variety of components are manufactured to enhance the handling performance of cars in both street and motorsports applications. Some of these products will allow easier, quicker, more accurate suspension adjustments, enabling improved performance. Other products reduce compliance and flex in the suspension and chassis, providing improved responsiveness to driver control inputs and better performance.

The flip side of these products is the increase in noise and ride harshness

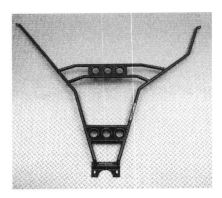

An engine bay brace like this Hotchkis Performance brace for a Monte Carlo increases chassis rigidity and helps performance. *Hotchkis Tuning*

arm moves 1 inch, but the mounting link of the antiroll bar moves only 1/2 inch, the motion ratio is 0.50. And like the wheel rate of a spring, the motion ratio is squared to determine the bar rate acting at the wheel. The ratio is squared because of the distance difference and the leverage reduction.

This strut tower brace made by Autobahn Design is on a VW Passat. *James Brown*

Eibach makes strut tower braces for several applications. Braces like this reduce flex between the strut towers and improve handling responsiveness and performance. *Eibach Springs*

in varying degrees, depending upon the nature and design of the product. For vehicles used only in competition, noise and harshness are not issues. For the street, some excellent compromises exist, allowing significant performance and response improvements without excessive increases in noise and harshness. Let's look at these product categories in more detail.

Suspension Bushings and Mounts

Suspension bushings are used to mount suspension components to the chassis of a vehicle. Rubber and other compliant materials are used in stock vehicles to isolate road noise and ride harshness from passengers. Racecars use solid metal or other rigid materials to reduce compliance and improve responsiveness with no consideration to comfort.

The best compromise for street vehicles and even cars used for both highway and motorsports applications is urethane bushings. They are quite rigid but maintain reasonable noise levels and offer just enough compliance to keep your teeth from rattling out on those bumpy roads and interstate highways.

Polyurethane bushings are available for many, if not most, street applications. For every soft bushing you replace in the suspension system, responsiveness and performance will

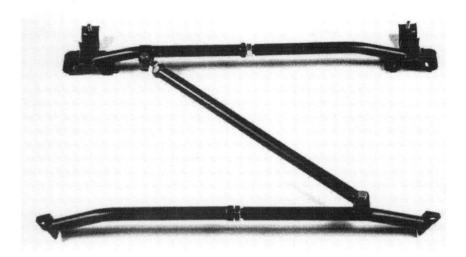

This subframe connector from Autotech Sport Tuning increases chassis rigidity by strengthening the mount from the subframe to the chassis. *Autotech Sport Tuning*

Strut and Chassis Braces

A variety of strut tower braces and chassis stiffeners are available for a wide range of vehicle applications. The worst form of compliance in a vehicle is chassis/body flex. When the chassis flexes, not only is performance and responsiveness hurt, but the chassis becomes a very large undamped spring that is nearly impossible to tune. This flex also causes premature wear to the chassis structure.

Many of today's vehicles lack sufficient chassis rigidity for performance

This camber plate from Hotchkis Performance is on a late model Mustang and can also be used to adjust caster. *Hotchkis Tuning*

improve. Polyurethane is used in suspensions for shock absorber bushings, suspension bump stops, radius/strut arm bushings, coil spring isolators, damper donuts, leaf spring pads, torque arm bushings, and rack-and-pinion bushings.

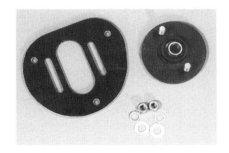

A camber plate for a strut suspension allows quick, easy adjustment of camber. This allows quick fine-tuning or change from a street setup to a motorsports application.

As with the suspension systems, other mounts and bushings are available for the driveline, including the engine and transmission. Mounts are also available for the body. The most readily available bushings and mounts are made from polyurethane. Polyurethane motor and transmission mounts will isolate vibrations, but greatly reduce compliance and mount twisting under the torque loads of acceleration and braking.

Replacing stock rubber mounts and bushings for any form of competition or combination street/competition vehicle is desirable from a performance, wear, reliability, and safety standpoint. Even with stock horsepower, today's ultra-high-performance and race-compound DOT tires make so much traction that damage to motor and transmission mounts can occur during hard acceleration, especially launches, and limit braking. Stiffer, stronger bushing and mounts will eliminate the problem of stock rubber parts and improve performance.

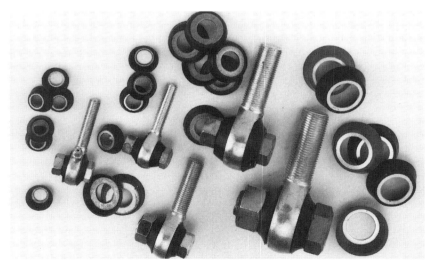

Rod ends are a great way to make control arms adjustable. These rod ends use dirt covers to keep the ball and socket free from damaging grit.

Here is a rod end used on the upper link of a rear suspension on a showroom stock racecar. Rear camber angle is quickly adjusted with this setup.

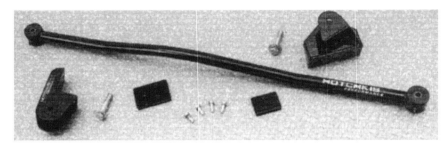

This panhard bar is used to laterally position the solid rear axle on a rear-drive car. The panhard bar allows vertical movement of the axle, but keeps it from moving sideways during suspension travel. Many trucks and rear drive cars use panhard bars to locate the rear axle assembly laterally. This Hotchkis Performance panhard bar is for a Chevy truck. *Hotchkis Tuning*

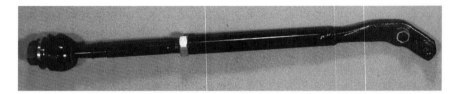

This is an adjustable drag strut used as part of the lower front control arm on a Nissan 240Z. The adjustable link allows caster adjustments.

and motorsports applications. A wide range of bolt-on strut tower braces and other chassis stiffeners are readily available. These products will greatly reduce chassis flex and improve performance. The addition of a roll bar, or especially a roll cage, will add even more chassis rigidity to a vehicle for any motorsports activity. The increase in driver safety is also a major plus for roll bars and roll cages.

Camber Adjusters

While many cars have some form of camber adjustment built into the front suspension and fewer have rear camber adjustments, most of these stock systems are cumbersome and time-consuming. Being able to quickly and accurately adjust camber is important for high-performance applications and crucial for motorsports. A convenient camber adjustment for dual-purpose cars allows a different setting for the street and for competition.

The most common camber adjuster is the camber plate, made primarily for strut-equipped vehicles. Other types of camber adjusters include spacers, adjustable A arms, and eccentric bushings.

Spherical Bearings and Rod Ends

The ultimate way to eliminate compliance and improve responsiveness in a competition car is the use of spherical

bearings and rod ends throughout the suspension system. These bearings are very rigid and allow angular movement with little free play. They also transmit vibration and noise very effectively, making them less than desirable for any kind of street application.

Panhard Bars and Lateral Locating Devices

Solid axles, like most rear axles on older American vehicles and some front-wheel-drive cars, require some means of lateral location. That is, some device to prevent side-to-side motion. In most cases, a Panhard bar is used (see illustration). Other devices include the Watt's linkage and the Jacob's ladder.

In all cases, the devices allow the axle free vertical movement but no lateral movement. The Panhard bar is the most common. In stock applications, it uses rubber bushings, which allow compliance and considerable lateral displacement during cornering at the limits of traction, especially with sticky tires and modified suspension. Solid bushings or rod ends on competition cars and polyurethane bushings for the street will eliminate or minimize the compliance.

This spacer for a bolt-on steering arm is used to eliminate bump steer, which occurs on some cars after the suspension is lowered.

Some cars equipped with strut suspensions do not have adequate suspension travel in bump when lowered significantly. This strut has been shortened, allowing more suspension travel with the lower ride height.

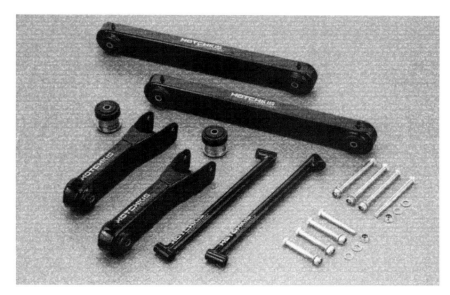

Rear control arm kits like this one from Hotchkis Performance improve strength and geometry, both important to improving handling performance. *Hotchkis Tuning*

 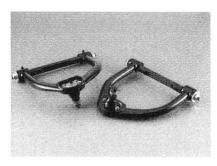

Aftermarket front control arms increase strength and improve geometry, often reducing camber gain. The arm on the left is for a Honda from the Progress Group. The photo on the right shows an upper control arm for an early Chevelle from Hotchkis. *Progress Group; Hotchkis Performance*

Drag Struts

Some vehicles use drag struts on the front suspension, usually as part of the lower control arm. Drag struts are often adjustable, allowing an easy and quick means of changing caster. Aftermarket adjustable drag struts are available for some applications. Unless flex is an issue, aftermarket drag struts will offer little in performance gains, but the added convenience of caster adjustment is worth considering.

Suspension Control Arms

Many companies make suspension control arms, both upper and lower A-arms for front suspension and trailing arms for the rear suspension, depending upon the application. In most cases, these aftermarket arms are stronger and often lighter than the stock components. Lighter suspension components reduce unsprung weight, which improves control of the tire contact patch over bumps. In some cases, the aftermarket arms are adjustable where the original equipment arms are not.

Limited-Slip Differentials

A standard differential allows the drive wheels to rotate at different speeds so that drag is reduced during cornering. The stock differential directs torque to the least-loaded tire, allowing wheelspin to occur earlier than is desirable. This is a big issue when launching a car from a standing start in drag racing or autocrossing. It is also an issue exiting slow- and medium-speed corners when the inside tire is still unloaded and can easily spin when the regular differential sends it more torque. A front driver has a bigger problem than a rear driver because weight transfer during acceleration is off the front tires.

Many oval track cars use a spool to lock the left and right rear-drive wheels together. This creates high cornering drag but helps with acceleration off the turns. This technique is not desirable for road racing, autocrossing, or drag racing and is plain dangerous for the highway.

The best solution is a limited-slip differential that transmits more torque to the tire with more traction but still allows a high degree of freewheeling during cornering. This reduces drag but greatly improves traction during launches and corner exits.

There are several types of limited-slip differentials. Many performance vehicles are equipped with them from the factory, and several brands are available for competition. Some are adjustable, allowing earlier lock-up of the differential clutches. In most cases, they greatly enhance performance. If one drive wheel is spinning easily on your car, consider a limited-slip differential.

One of the most important items for improved performance is a limited-slip differential. They allow harder acceleration on a launch or exiting a corner by sending more torque to the wheel with more traction. This is a Quaiffe unit from Autotech Sport Tuning. *Autotech Sport Tuning*

Chapter Five
Suspension Alignment

You just spent $3,000 on wheels, tires, sport springs, and shocks. With great anticipation, you take your car out on your favorite canyon road for the first time after installing the new parts. While the car feels stiff and responsive, the handling improvement is not what you anticipated and you are disappointed.

This is common, but often there is a simple cure for the problem. In virtually every case, the suspension needs to be aligned after installing a suspension package. Lowering a car often causes camber and toe settings and caster to change. For most people, using a good alignment shop that understands high-performance suspensions is

While suspension alignment is crucial on the race track, it is also important on the street for safety, performance, and reliability. Anytime you modify the suspension, the alignment should be checked and reset if necessary. *Ford Motorsports UK*

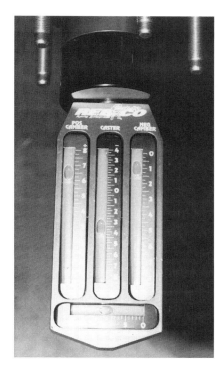

A bubble caster/camber gauge is the most accurate way to adjust caster and camber.

the easiest way to get your car back to proper alignment settings. If you prefer to do it yourself, follow the procedures and use the settings found in the factory repair manual for your vehicle.

For most street applications, using the factory camber, toe, and caster settings is best. We'll look at the effects of changes for each specific setting later. For competition, different settings will offer improved performance on the track, but tire wear could be excessive and straight line stability compromised for street driving. Let's examine each of the specific settings that require attention.

Setting Camber

Camber is the tilt of the tire when viewed from the front of the car. Positive camber means the top of the tire is tilted away from the car. Negative camber means the top is tilted in. Camber angles should be measured on all wheels, though with a solid rear axle system, camber cannot be adjusted. But many independent rear suspension

cars can be adjusted easily. Some static negative camber is beneficial for maximum cornering traction. The downside of this is increased tire wear on the inside edge of the tread. For this reason, using more than 1/2 degree negative camber on the street is not a good idea. For competition, up to 3 degrees is acceptable, but greater angles will cause a reduction in straight-line braking performance and acceleration, especially launches in drag racing and autocrossing.

Most factory specifications for camber indicate an angle of 0 to 1/2 degree positive. For street performance improvements, use up to 1/2 degree negative camber.

For motorsports applications, the best way to set camber is to monitor tire temperatures. The goal is to have nearly equal temperatures across the surface of the tire, with the inside edge of the tire about 5 to 10 degrees F hotter. This indicates the perfect camber angle for your application and track conditions.

To set camber, refer to the factory repair manual for your vehicle or the instructions for aftermarket camber adjusting products. A bubble caster/camber gauge is the best tool for setting camber, but the key is to use tire temperatures to tune and then measure the camber angle so that the settings can be repeated.

Setting Caster

Caster is the inclination of the steering axis in the front when viewed from the side. See the accompanying diagrams for a better idea of caster angles. Caster adds stability to the steering, and if it's off, either steering effort increases too much, or the car loses stability and wanders, especially on grooved interstate highways and on longitudinal expansion strips. For this reason, caster should always be set to factory specs for the highway and should never vary more than 1 degree in either direction for motorsports applications using stock control arms and spindles. A bubble caster gauge is the best tool to use for setting caster. To set caster, refer to the factory repair manual for your vehicle.

Setting Toe

While camber is a displacement of the top of the tire in or out, as viewed from the front, toe refers to the relationship between the front edges of the front or rear tires when viewed from above. Toe-in means the front edges of the tires are closer together than the rear edges. The opposite is toe-out. Both front and rear tires should be checked for toe. Most cars need a small amount of rear toe-in for straight-line stability. Most manufacturers spec toe-in at the front as well for better steering

An angle finder, either a bubble style or an electronic gauge, works well for measuring camber angles and can be used for caster.

The Laser String from Advanced Racing Technologies is one of the must useful alignment tools available, allowing accurate and easy measurements of rear axle alignment, toe, chassis squareness, and many other characteristics affecting performance. *Advanced Racing Technologies*

feel. For motorsports applications, toe-out is usually better for steering response at corner turn-in.

Toe is usually measured in inches or millimeters at the edge of the wheel rim or on the tire tread. The amount of toe is the difference between the front and rear measurements on a given rim or tire from the exact same line, such as a tread groove. If the forward-side measurement is larger, toe-out is present. Toe is adjusted through lengthening or shortening the tie rods. It is best to make half the adjustment at each tie rod when possible rather than a single large adjustment on one tie-rod. Altering tie rod lengths can cause the steering wheel to rotate off center. The absolute best way to measure toe is with a laser toe gauge, especially for motorsports. Other methods are outlined later in this chapter.

For the highway, use factory toe specs front and rear. For motorsports, a small degree of toe-out can be used in the front. The amount depends upon how tight the turns are. More toe-out is effective on a tight autocross course, but less would be used on a fast road course. On the rear, unless the factory specs for your vehicle say otherwise, toe-in should be used.

Toe Recommendations

All measurements here are in inches and measured at the rim face, which is 15 to 18 inches. If you measure at the tire tread, which has a larger diameter than the rim, use a slightly larger number, about 1/32 to 1/16 inch more. For rear suspension with toe adjustments, toe should be about 1/8 inch. More will cause tire drag and reduce performance and increase tire wear.

For front suspensions, use 1/16 to 1/8 inch for road courses, rallying, and import drag front-drive cars. For autocrossing, use 1/8 inch to 3/16 inch. If you drive your vehicle to the track, reset the toe for competition and return to factory specs for highway driving to reduce wear and improve stability on the highway. Front-drive cars often respond favorably to more front toe-out than rear-drive cars. In any case, be conservative with toe settings.

Rear Axle Alignment

If your vehicle has adjustable camber or toe, follow the above suggestions and refer to your factory repair manual for procedures. If you have a solid rear axle, measure camber and toe. Up to a 1/2 degree per side of negative camber is acceptable, and up to 1/8 total toe-in is acceptable. Greater amounts or any toe-out or positive camber will cause problems and the axle should be

This laser gauge from Advanced Racing Technologies is used to measure chassis and axle squareness. *Advanced Racing Technologies*

straightened by an experienced body shop or racecar fabricator.

Bump Steer

Bump steer is unwanted mechanical steering input that can cause the car to pull in a direction contrary to the driver's desired path. It occurs, as the name implies, over bumps due to toe changes during suspension travel. Bump steer is caused by a conflict between steering geometry and suspension geometry. If you plot the path of the front suspension in bump and rebound travel and plot the path of the tie rods during travel, they should be identical for zero bump steer.

Often when a car is lowered, the geometry between the suspension and the tie rods changes, causing some steering wheel pull over bumps while going straight. If the steering wheel jerks hard over one-wheel bumps, then the problem should be addressed for safety. In motorsports, bump steer causes tire scrub, reduces straight-line speed, and hurts cornering performance at the limits of tire adhesion.

Measuring bump steer requires measuring toe at various points in bump and rebound travel. To do this you must remove the springs and shocks (just springs on a strut suspension) so that the suspension can be moved easily through bump and rebound travel. Normally, toe is measured at ride height and again at 1 inch and 2 inches of both bump and rebound travel. If there is any difference in toe measurements from ride height during bump or rebound travel, then the vehicle will experience bump steer. A change of up to 1/8 inch at 2 inches of travel is a minor concern for street vehicles. For competition vehicles, any bump steer should be eliminated.

There are many different bump steer scenarios, and it is a very time-consuming problem to correct, often requiring fabrication and machining. The best way to correct bump steer problems is to work with an experienced race preparation shop.

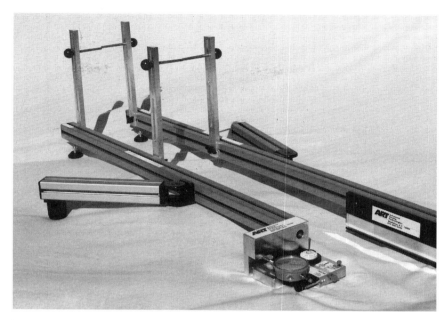
This is a laser toe gauge from Advanced Racing Technologies. This gauge is accurate to less than one minute of arc. *Advanced Racing Technologies*

Roll Steer

Roll steer is unwanted steering input from the rear of the vehicle during cornering. It occurs when there is rear toe change during bump or rebound travel. Roll steer is less likely than bump steer when a vehicle is lowered. It is measured the same way as bump steer and is equally difficult to correct.

Cheap Setup Tricks

Suspension setup is crucial to achieving peak handling performance. Some of the tools for this art, such as scales and laser alignment equipment,

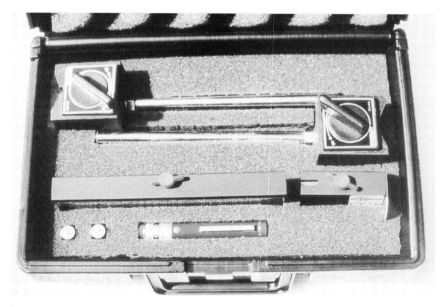
This Advanced Racing Technologies bump steer gauge makes measuring bump steer easy and accurate. *Advanced Racing Technologies*

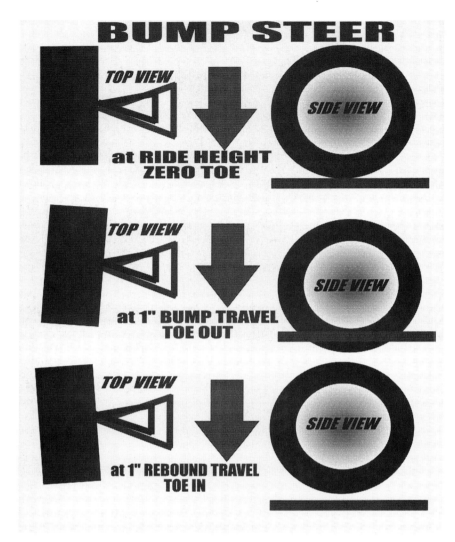

BUMP STEER

TOP VIEW

SIDE VIEW

at RIDE HEIGHT ZERO TOE

TOP VIEW

SIDE VIEW

at 1" BUMP TRAVEL TOE OUT

TOP VIEW

SIDE VIEW

at 1" REBOUND TRAVEL TOE IN

This illustration shows that bump steer is a change in toe during vertical wheel travel of the front suspension.

are very expensive. If you really need these tools, you may have to rent or borrow them. Fortunately, for less than $100, you can accomplish 99 percent of your suspension setup work. Then all you really need is a tire pyrometer (as low $99) and a stopwatch. Here's the list of what you will need:

- Machinist's rule
- Plumb bob
- Level
- Angle finder
- Tape measure
- Angle iron or plate (steel or aluminum)

1. Check Toe with String

A roll of survey string, available at any hardware store, is all you need to quickly check front toe. (Park the car on a level surface with the front wheels pointing straight.) The string must be held so that it passes around the outside of the rear tire, touching both the front and rear sidewall bulges at axle height. Unroll more string and, keeping it taut, slowly move the string until it just touches either the front or rear sidewall bulge of the front tire, again at axle height. Using a machinist's rule, measure the gap between the string and the sidewall it doesn't touch. This

measurement is the toe-out if the gap is at the rear, and toe-in if the gap is at the front. If the string does not contact both the front and rear bulge of the rear tire sidewall, or makes a slight bend off the front bulge of the rear sidewall, the rear axle is either offset or out of alignment. Keep in mind that this method will not work on racecars where the rear track width varies more than 1 inch from the front track width.

2. Check Front and Rear Toe with Plumb

Refer to the illustrations. First, put a true scribe mark around the tire. Then, place a piece of 1-inch masking tape on the floor where the plumb bobs will touch. Next, lay string with plumb bobs accurately over the scribe line so that the tips of the plumb bobs just clear the floor. Then let the plumb bobs stabilize and carefully mark the floor where the plumb bobs come to rest. Do this on both sides and use a tape measure to measure between the marks. This is a very accurate way to measure toe if the scribe lines are accurate.

An even more accurate way to do this is to use aluminum or steel angle iron that is 24 inches long. Carefully notch each end for the plumb bob string so that the notch is in exactly the same location at each end. Mount the angle iron to the brake rotor with either reversed lug nuts or clamps and level the angle iron. Mark the floor where the plumb bobs come to rest as above and repeat on the opposite side. Take measurements on the floor between the marks. You can also use this method to check rear axle housing toe.

3. Square the Box

The box formed by the steering arm, idler arm, and drag link must be square to avoid unwanted bump steer. The distance between pivot points of the steering must be measured accurately. Center the steering by rolling the car forward at least one full tire revolution. With a tape, measure between the steering arm and idler arm pivots at the mounted end pivot centers and at the drag link. They should be identical. Adjust if needed. Then measure the diagonals. They should also be equal. If the distance between pivots is equal, but the diagonals are unequal, something is bent. Take a close look.

4. Bump Steer

Bump steer is toe change during vertical wheel travel. You can use the same setup as in number 2 to measure bump steer. Just disconnect the spring and shock (with the chassis on stands) and use a jack to raise and lower the suspension. Start with the suspension at ride height and mark your piece of tape. This is your baseline. As you raise and lower the suspension, the marks will usually move inward with zero bump steer. If one end moves farther from the baseline than the other end, the vehicle will experience bump steer. The difference in measurements is the amount of bump steer. If the front measurement is bigger, you have toe-out; if the rear is bigger you have toe-in. Plot the change at 1-inch increments for 3 inches of bump and 3 inches of rebound travel at each front wheel.

5. Caster

Use an angle finder on a vertical location on the front spindles. This may not be completely accurate for actual caster angle, but it allows you to get back to the initial setting after you have modified your suspension or made another change.

6. Camber

Camber should really be set by tire temps, so knowing a camber angle in advance is not important. But once you get the tire temps right, you need to know the camber angle so that you can repeat that setup at the track. Make sure the car is on level ground before measuring. You can use a straightedge against the tire with an angle finder (be sure to avoid the raised letters on the sidewall), or place the angle finder on the upper control arm.

One cause of bump steer is steering links out of alignment. Squaring the box formed by the steering arm, idler arm, and the drag link will reduce or eliminate bump steer. See the section in this chapter.

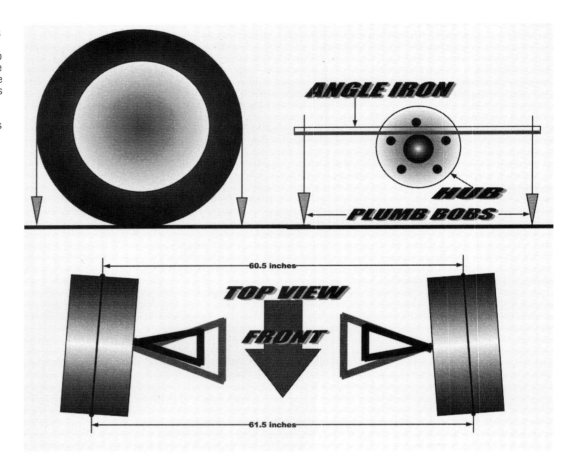

Its angle is directly related to the camber angle at that wheel.

7. Panhard Bar Setting

If your car has a panhard bar on the rear suspension, use either an angle finder on the panhard bar for an angle, or scribe a line around the adjuster on the slider tube (if you have one) and use that as your baseline. A machinist's rule can then be used to measure above or below the baseline.

8. Cross-weight

While scales are the easiest way to do this, the cross-weight is determined by ride heights. If the ride height is changed, the cross-weight changes. Changing cross-weight is easy to accomplish with adjustable spring perches or coil-over shocks. If you do not have access to scales for a baseline, set the rear ride height to the measure-ment recommended by the suspension package manufacturer and level side to side. Set the front slightly lower but also level side to side. At the track you can tune the chassis by changing ride heights in very small amounts to a full turn while trying to keep any single corner of the chassis from getting too high or low. Keep notes and do this until the car handles the same in left and right turns. Recheck the ride heights and now you have a setup that works. It is a lot more time consuming, but you don't need scales to get there.

9. Rear Axle Alignment

For a solid rear axle suspension, a simple tape measure is all you need. Measure from a lateral frame rail forward of the axle housing to the rear axle housing. The trick is finding a spot on each side of the housing that is square. Better yet, drop a plumb bob from the hub on the axle centerline on each side and draw a line through each mark. Measure from the line to an identical spot on the left and right sides of the lateral frame rail. Now you have a very accurate measurement. The rear axle housing is out of alignment if the measurements are not identical.

10. Brake Bias

Brake bias is best set on the track with an observer watching for wheel lock-up at one end of the car first. Just use old tires. You can get in the ballpark with a torque wrench. With the car on stands, have someone apply the brakes until one end locks up. Use the torque wrench on a wheel lug and measure the torque it takes to turn the wheel. Apply more pressure until the other end just locks up. Check the torque at the first end again. The front

should lock up first, and due to weight transfer the front should require some amount of torque higher than the rear. Asphalt needs more front bias than dirt. Test the bias on the straightaway with an observer before you run at speed on the track.

11. Scaling

You need to know what your car weighs and the corner weights. If you don't have scales, try to use the track scales, or borrow old grain scales. If all else fails, use local official truck scales, so that you have a place to start with each corner separately at the same spot on the scale platform. The vehicle should be weighed with the driver on board.

12. Rear-End Trueness

On solid rear axle vehicles, it is important to know if the rear axle is straight, or has camber or toe. We checked toe in number 2. Use the angle finder on the brake rotor for camber. Be sure the car is level on jack stands. A little toe, up to 1/8 inch, and a little negative camber, up to 3/16 inch, is sufficient. More of either, or any toe out or positive camber, requires that the rear axle housing be straightened.

13. Wheel and Brake Rotor Runout

Clamp a scribe or pointed punch to a weighted (for stability) jack stand. Place the end of the scribe against the wheel rim at the bead or against a brake rotor. Rotate the wheel or rotor until you find the high spot and position the scribe. Rotate the wheel or rotor until you find the low spot and use a machinist's rule to measure the gap. That is the amount of runout. Check with the wheel or rotor manufacturer about runout tolerances. Too much wheel runout will have an effect similar to bump steer, and rotor runout will cause brake pad kickback, which you can often feel in the brake pedal under hard braking. Rotor runout hurts braking performance.

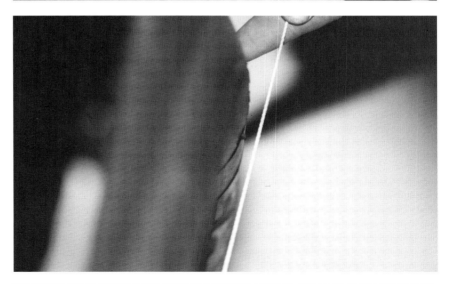

Toe settings can be measured with string against the tire sidewalls. This is not an accurate measurement, but can be used at an event for a quick check of toe settings. See accompanying text

Chapter Six
Weighing, Crossweights, and Tuning with Crossweights

The weight of a car is a key factor to its performance. While less of an issue for street cars, getting a competition vehicle to the lowest possible weight, at least the lowest weight allowed by the rules, is paramount to success. But just as important is the car's weight distribution. Getting the weight where it does the most good, or has the least ill effect, is also crucial to performance. Most of this chapter is focused on competition, but to derive the highest degree of performance from a street car, the same principles apply.

The Importance of Weight Distribution

Your car is really fast in right-hand turns, but understeers in left turns. If you get the car into neutral in left turns, it oversteers in right turns. You've tried springs, shocks, different bars, and neutralizing the antiroll bar, but nothing seems to work. Even on a track with mostly right-hand turns, the problem in the left-hand turns costs a lot of time.

Several different setup parameters could have caused this situation, yet the likely culprit is excessive crossweight. One of the most important aspects of car setup is the static weight distribution and the crossweight percentage. It is important to weigh your car and get the four individual corner

Weighing a racecar is mandatory both to meet minimum weight requirements, but also to set weight distribution and crossweight percentage. Electronic scales are the easiest way to do this.

Electronic scales not only weigh the car but calculate a variety of weights and percentages.

weights. The most effective way to do this is with electronic corner weight scales, whether you purchase them or borrow them. You can also use public scales by placing one wheel at a time on the weighing platform. However you get it, this is important information, and understanding how to use it is even more critical.

Static Weight Distribution

Static weight distribution is the weight resting on each tire contact patch with the car at rest exactly the way it will be driven—with the driver in the car, all fluids topped up, and the fuel load such that, for competition, the car meets your association's minimum weight rule at the designated time, usually after an event. The car should be at minimum weight, using ballast as needed to make the proper weight.

When working with static weight distribution, we use two percentages to analyze the car's corner weights. The left-side weight percent and rear weight percent tell us all we need to know about the setup relative to the weight distribution. The left-side weight percentage is found by adding the left front weight to the left rear weight and dividing the sum by the total weight. The rear weight percentage is found in the same way: add the left rear and the right rear weight together and divide the sum by the total weight. Many electronic scales will perform the calculations for you.

For road racing and autocrossing, the ideal left-side weight percentage is

50 percent. This makes the cornering force balanced from left to right and offers the best performance overall, though many cars cannot make it due to driver offset. The rear weight percentage for road racing and autocrossing is less definite. The more power a car has, the more static weight over the drive wheels, up to a point, helps acceleration off the corners. Additionally, it is much more difficult to change rear percentage, since rear weight is mostly a design function. It still pays to be thoughtful about weight placement fore and aft in your car. The only way to change the static weight distribution percentages is to physically move weight around in the car. Jacking weight by changing ride heights will not alter the left side or the rear percentages.

Crossweight Percentage

Crossweight percentage compares the diagonal weight totals to the total car weight. To calculate crossweight percentage, add the *right front weight* to the *left rear weight* and divide the sum by the total weight of the car. Crossweight is also called wedge. If the percentage is over 50 percent, the car has wedge; below 50 percent the car has reverse wedge. More wedge means that the car will likely understeer more in a left turn. The advantage to wedge is that the left rear tire carries more load, so the car drives off the turns better. But in a right turn, the opposite occurs and the handling is worse. In almost all cases, the loss of cornering performance in one direction is greater than the gain in the other direction. The optimum crossweight percentage for road racing and autocrossing is a very narrow range, from 49.5 percent to 50.5 percent.

On oval-track cars, crossweight is usually used in conjunction with stagger (where the right rear tire is larger in

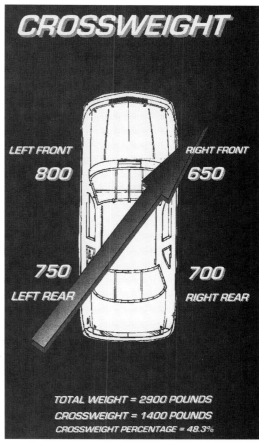

This illustration defines crossweight.

The scale platforms must be level with each other to get accurate wheel weights and percentages.

circumference than the left rear tire) to balance handling. More stagger usually loosens the handling (increases oversteer) in left turns, so more crossweight is used to tighten up the handling. But stagger is not a good idea on a road course or autocross.

One of the problems with crossweight is that it will change the handling balance from a left to a right turn. This can make maneuvering in traffic difficult, even dangerous. That's why, on a road course, the ideal crossweight percentage is 50 percent. In the example at the beginning of this chap-ter, the car had a crossweight percentage less than 50 percent, probably off by at least 2 percent.

One of the keys to a good setup is using the correct procedure to weigh your racecar.

How to Weigh Racecars

Here are some points to remember when weighing your racecar:
- Make sure the floor is perfectly level; use shims under the scale pads if needed. Small angles can throw off your readings significantly.
- Set tire pressures first.

- Check stagger at each tire, even with radials for road racing and autocrossing.
- Put the driver weight in the car, preferably by using the actual driver.
- Use a load of fuel for where you want the car balanced, either at the start of the race, the end of the race, or an average between the two.
- Disconnect the shocks, when possible, and the antiroll bars.
- When making adjustments, use blocks the same height as your scale pads.
- Bounce the car at each corner to free the suspension from any bind, then roll it onto the scales.
- Make sure the tires are centered on the scales.
- Recheck air pressure often to ensure the ride heights stay consistent.

Setting Static Weight Distribution
- Check static weight before working on crossweight.
- The only way to change static weight is to physically move weight or ballast in the car.
- To increase left-side weight, move weight as far to the left as possible.
- To increase rear weight, move weight as far back as possible.
- Move ballast first, since it's easier, then you will have to move components such as the battery or fuel cell.
- It is best to get left-side weight to 50 percent when possible.
- Get the rear percentage close to 50 percent for rear-drive cars and close to 40 percent for front-drive cars. Too much front-weight percent can cause the car to become very unstable at speed, a problem for front-drive drag racecars.

Setting Crossweight

The weight on each corner of the car has a direct effect on handling. Crossweight, that is, the comparison of the weight resting on diagonal pairs of tires, determines the handling balance in left versus right turns. Adjusting this

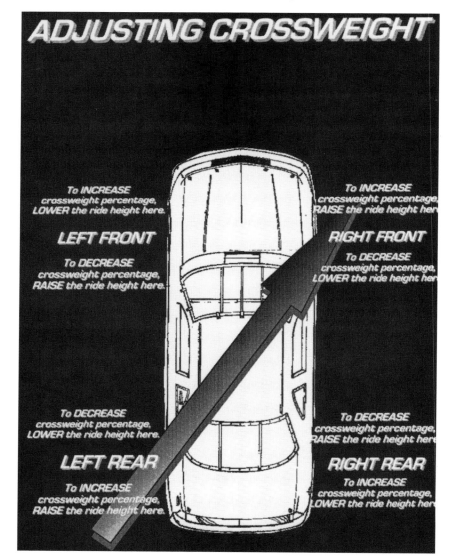

This illustration shows the variety of weight percentages used for setup and chassis tuning with corner weights.

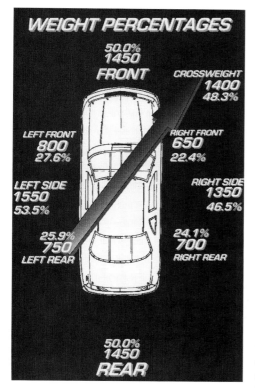

WEIGHT PERCENTAGES

50.0%
1450
FRONT

CROSSWEIGHT
1400
48.3%

LEFT FRONT
800
27.6%

RIGHT FRONT
650
22.4%

LEFT SIDE
1550
53.5%

RIGHT SIDE
1350
46.5%

25.9%
750
LEFT REAR

24.1%
700
RIGHT REAR

50.0%
1450
REAR

When adjusting crossweight percentage, it is always best to make four small changes, one at each corner, rather than one or two large changes. You will raise one diagonal and lower the other. Making four small changes minimizes ride height changes at any one corner, maintaining a more level chassis, and better suspension geometry. To raise or lower the ride height at any given corner, raise or lower the chassis relative to the ground. This can be done with spring perches, spring height, or spring spacers.

so that the diagonal weights are equal will provide the same handling for left and right turns. The way to change crossweight is to change the ride heights of the car. By changing one ride height—the height of the chassis to the ground at one corner of the car—the crossweight is altered. This is similar to shortening or lengthening one leg of a chair or table: more or less weight is thereby forced to rest on the other legs. The most weight rests on the longest leg.

On a car, raising the ride height on a corner of the car forces more static weight onto that corner. It also puts more weight on the diagonally opposite corner and removes weight from

the two other corners. Lowering a corner takes weight away from that corner and the diagonally opposite corner and adds weight to the two remaining corners. By carefully adjusting ride heights, the ideal crossweight percentage can be obtained.

For road racing, autocrossing, time trials, track days, and rallying, 50 percent crossweight is ideal. Anything less than 49.5 percent or greater than 50.5 percent will adversely affect handling in one direction, while helping in the other. As we have seen in the tire traction chapter, however, the gain in one direction will not be enough to compensate for the loss in the other (due to the nature of traction relative to vertical loads on the tire). For drag racing, it is still ideal to have the crossweights at 50 percent for straight-line stability and optimum launch, but it's just as important that the drive wheels have equal weights in the static state. Following are some tips for setting crossweights:

- Once static weight percentages are set, work on crossweight percentages.
- You cannot change the left or rear percentages by jacking weight around in the car, but this will change crossweight.
- Changing the ride height at any corner will change the crossweight percentage.
- If you raise the ride height at a given corner (put a turn in or add a round of wedge), the weight on that corner will increase, as will the weight on the diagonally opposite corner. The other two corners will lose weight.
- If you lower the ride height at a given corner, that corner will lose weight as will the diagonally opposite corner. The other two corners will gain weight.

- To add weight to a given corner, raise the ride height at that corner, or lower the ride height at an adjacent corner. For example, if your initial setup is 52 percent crossweight, and you want 50 percent crossweight, lowering the right front or left rear corner will decrease crossweight percentage. You could also raise the left front or right rear ride heights to do the same thing.
- It is best to make small changes at each corner, instead of a big change at one corner. This keeps the ride heights as close to ideal as possible. In the above example, to go from 52 percent to 50 percent crossweight, try lowering the right-front and left-rear one-half turn on the spring perch, and raise the left front and right rear the same amount.
- Always record the crossweights and ride heights for reference at the race track, if changes are needed.
- Measure control arm angles after each change. These angles are another way to set the suspension for the desired ride height and crossweight percentage.
- Measuring the distance from the ground to an inner-suspension arm pivot point will also accomplish the above goal.
- Remember that stagger changes, tire pressure changes, and spring changes will change the ride height and alter the crossweight percentage.

Changes at the Track
- Make small changes at the track, and make only one change at a time.
- If the car understeers or oversteers in only one direction, check the crossweight percentage.
- Good handling balance is essential in competitive motorsports. Setting static weight distribution and adjusting crossweight percentage is one way to ensure good handling.

Chapter Seven
Wheels and Tires

Aftermarket wheels perform three important functions. They enhance the look of a vehicle, they allow a vehicle to be personalized, and they usually (and should) improve performance. While wheels offer the easiest installation of any component in the suspension system, they are actually the most difficult product to choose because there are so many options and compatibility issues to address. In addition to size and fit within the wheelwell, the offset must be correct, the lug bolt holes must be compatible with the lug bolts or studs, and the centerbore of the wheel must match the hub for proper fit.

Many wheel manufacturers and retailers offer excellent advice on wheel fit. I've worked with Tire Rack personnel for more than a decade and have great confidence in their knowledge and skill: Tire Rack provided most of the information in this chapter. After all, why reinvent the wheel?

Plus Sizing

Plus sizing your wheels and tires may be the simplest way to improve both the performance and appearance of your vehicle. By using a larger-diameter

Custom wheels not only add to the look of a car, but allow a greater tire selection and improve performance potential. These Zender Monza wheels on an Audi A4 Quattro are 18 inch by 8.5 inches wide with a 35-millimeter offset, allowing the use of BFG g-Force KD 225-40 ZR18 ultra-high-performance tires.

wheel with a lower-profile tire it's possible to maintain the diameter of the stock tire, keeping odometer and speedometer changes negligible. By using a tire with a shorter sidewall, you gain quickness in steering response and better lateral stability. The visual appeal is obvious: most wheels look better than the sidewall of the tire.

Alloy and Steel Wheels

While many people choose alloy wheels for their beauty, there are equally important performance benefits to be derived, including reduced unsprung weight compared to steel wheels.

This is one of the most critical factors affecting a vehicle's road-holding ability. Unsprung weight is that portion of a vehicle that is not supported by the suspension (that is, wheels, tires, and brakes) and therefore most susceptible to road shock and cornering forces. By reducing unsprung weight, alloy wheels provide more precise steering input and improved "turning in" characteristics.

Improved Acceleration and Braking

By reducing the weight of the vehicle's rotational mass, alloy wheels provide more responsive acceleration and braking.

Added Rigidity

The added strength of a quality alloy wheel can significantly reduce wheel/tire deflection in cornering. This is particularly critical with an automobile equipped with high-performance tires where lateral forces may approach 1.0-g.

Increased Brake Cooling

The metals in alloy wheels are excellent heat conductors, improving dissipation of brake heat and reducing the risk of brake fade under demanding conditions. Additionally, alloy wheels can be designed to allow more cooling air to flow over the brakes.

Wheel Construction

Aluminum alloy wheels come in one-, two-, and three-piece construction types, with most being one-piece wheels. One-piece wheels are cast, forged, or roll forged in a mold in one complete section. Two-piece wheels have a separate inner section and outer section. They are either bolted or welded together.

Always be cautious of wheels that are just welded together, as they seem not always to be as round as one-piece wheels. The two-piece wheels that are bolted together tend to be of high quality. Three-piece wheels use not only a separate center, but also have two outer sections, the inner and outer rim halves. These three-piece modular wheels use aircraft-quality bolts to hold them together, and many of them use forged components to reduce weight, while improving strength. The use of three-piece wheels allows the manufacturer greater flexibility in offering many wheel models-even in small quantities.

Manufacturing

The performance of an alloy wheel is a direct result of the manufacturing technique employed.

Low-Pressure/Gravity Casting

In this most basic method, molten metal is poured from a vat directly into a mold and allowed to harden.

Counter-Pressure Casting

This sophisticated casting method draws the molten alloy up into the mold via a very strong vacuum, helping it maintain a consistent temperature and leaving the impurities behind. The result is an extremely nonporous wheel of uniform density providing superior strength.

High-Counter-Pressure Molding (HCM)

HCM is a manufacturing technique that exhibits approximately the same strength characteristics as forging at little more than cast-wheel price. This unique manufacturing method is used in the BBS RX design.

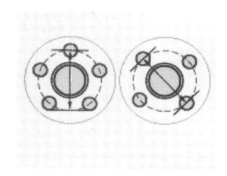

The diagram indicates the proper measuring methods for wheel bolt pattern diameters. Six-lug wheels are measured like the four-lug wheels. *Tire Rack*

Forging

The most advanced method of manufacturing wheels, forging involves compressing a billet of aluminum into a wheel with a combination of heat and as much as 14 million pounds of pressure. The result is a wheel that is up to three times stronger and as much as 20 percent lighter than a conventional cast wheel. Roll forging is a variation of forging where a rough cast rim is pressed into its final shape while rolling. Roll-forged wheels require less material thickness than cast wheels, which reduces the weight while maintaining strength. The roll-forging manufacturing method is used to produce the BBS RSII.

Finishes and Care

Alloy wheels, especially clear-coated styles, require special care in cleaning. Try to avoid commercial wheel cleaners by using the same soap and water you use to wash the car. Some wheel manufacturers are so adamant about the potential damage from wheel cleaners that their use voids the finish warranty of the wheel. The easiest way to combat brake dust and road salt is to clean the wheels often, especially the front wheels, which generate more brake-pad wear. Both brake dust and road salt can eventually damage the wheels' finish. If kept clean, the finish of your alloys will be good for the life of your car. Small

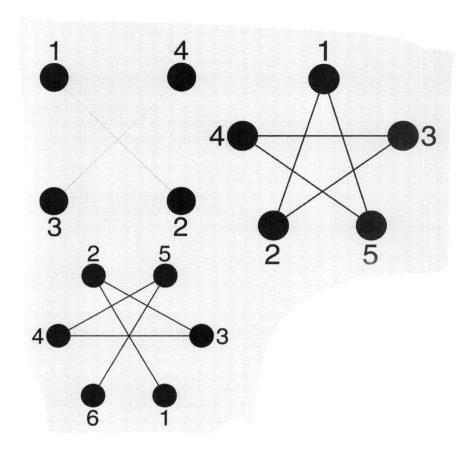

These illustrations show the proper torque sequence for various lug bolt patterns. *Tire Rack*

chips in the clear coat should be touched up with a little clear enamel to seal the finish, and an occasional light coat of wax will make cleaning easier.

Bolt Pattern

The bolt pattern or bolt circle is the diameter of an imaginary circle formed by the centers of the wheel lugs. Wheels may use four-, five-, six-, or eight-lug holes. A bolt circle of 4x100 would indicate a four-lug pattern on a circle with a diameter of 100 millimeters.

Centerbore

The centerbore of a wheel is the size of the machined hole on the back of the wheel that centers the wheel properly on the hub of the car. This hole is machined to match the hub exactly so the wheels are precisely posi-tioned, minimizing the chance of vibration. With a hubcentric wheel, the lug hardware does not support the weight of the vehicle; it merely holds the wheel against the hub, which bears the weight. Some wheels use high-quality, forged centering rings that lock into place in the back of the wheel. This is an acceptable alternative to a centerbore.

If you have nonhubcentric (lug-centric) wheels, they should be torqued correctly with the vehicle weight off the wheel, so they center properly. If you leave the wheel on the ground, the weight of the vehicle can push the wheel off-center slightly while you're tightening down the lugs.

Torque

Wheels should be tightened with a torque wrench whenever possible. Use the settings recommended by the man-ufacturer, or if they aren't available, use the settings below. The amount of torque needed is related to the size of the hardware. If you're installing new wheels, recheck them after driving on them for a day or two because expan-sion and contraction from temperature changes may affect lug tightness.

Offset

The offset of a wheel is the dis-tance from its hub-mounting surface to the centerline of the wheel. The off-set can be one of three types.

Zero Offset

The hub-mounting surface is even with the centerline of the wheel.

Positive

The hub-mounting surface is toward the outside of the wheel. Positive offset wheels are generally found on front-wheel-drive cars and newer rear-drive cars.

Negative

The hub-mounting surface is toward the back or brake side of the wheel centerline. "Deep dish" wheels typically have negative offset.

If the offset of the wheel is not correct for the car, the handling can be adversely affected. When the width of the wheel changes, the offset also changes numerically. If the offset were to stay the same while you added width, the additional width would be split evenly between the inside and outside. For most cars, this won't work correctly. Wheels are sized by the orig-inal manufacturer to provide sufficient room between the tire and the fender well. Adding width to the outside of the wheel will likely cause the tire to extend beyond the fenderwell or press up against it. Tire Rack and other tire and wheel service companies have tested thousands of different vehicles for proper fit, and their extensive databases should be useful in finding a wheel that matches your specifications.

Hardware Size	Torque in Ft/Lbs
10 millimeter	45–55
12 millimeter	70–80
14 millimeter	85–90
7/16 inch	70–80
1/2 inch	75–85
9/16 inch	135–145

Alloys on the Track

Today many car clubs and professional driving schools allow drivers to learn more about high-performance driving as they run their street cars (with relatively few modifications) on the same race tracks where the pros compete. While it's common sense that track use will increase the wear on a car's tires, brakes, and shocks, there are less obvious critical components that also wear out, such as the wheels! Wheels fatigue.

Because wheels are so critical to the driver's safety, top racing teams visually inspect their wheels at the track, monitor the total number of hours they are used, and crack test them periodically. Any wheel that shows signs of fatigue or age is discarded and replaced. Indy Car sanctioning bodies, and others, require that their race participants' wheels meet strict standards when new and that previously used wheels be recertified before every 500-mile race.

Unfortunately, the same rigorous wheel inspection procedures are not typical for many driving enthusiasts who use their vehicles on the track. Wheels are so trouble-free that they are often overlooked. Over time, however, wheels that are subjected to high-stress track conditions can fail, and as you can imagine, suffering a disintegrating wheel going into a high-speed turn can pose life-threatening danger.

Wheel fatigue is caused by a combination of the frequency and magnitude of the stresses the wheel encounters. Small stresses can be accommodated for thousands of cycles, whereas large stresses accelerate the wheel's fatigue factor and significantly reduce the wheel's resistance to future damage and failure. So what is it about track use that reduces the life expectancy of wheels? Let's explore some of the important factors.

All wheels flex as they are driven through a corner. In normal street driving the amount of flex is minimal. However, since today's DOT-legal competition tires almost match the performance of yesterday's racing tires, every corner that is taken at the limit on the track causes significantly more flex. It's the combination of the extra tire grip and the resulting extra flex that fatigues wheels faster when used on the track. And don't forget that spins, running over the track edge

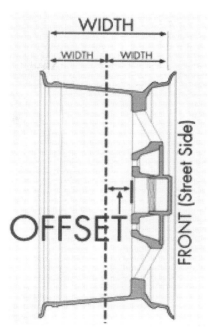

This diagram shows wheel offset. Here is positive offset, which most modern cars use. Negative offset would be present if the wheel hub flange was to the inside of the wheel centerline. *Tire Rack*

This is the proper way to measure wheel backspacing. If the backspace is more than half of the wheel's width, the offset is positive. It it's less than half, it's negative. The backspace less half the width of the wheel (in inches or millimeters) equals the wheel offset.

This Golf features Volk Racing SE37 forged aluminum 8-x18-inch wheels and 245/40R18 BF Goodrich G-Force TA KD tires.

hardware is correct for the vehicle and in good condition. Since almost all of today's cars are designed with hub-centric wheels, which transfer the vehicle's load from the center of the wheel to the car's hub (and allow the lug nuts/bolts to just hold the wheel against the hub), it is important to use hubcentric track wheels. If an aftermarket wheel requires special centering rings to fit it to the hub, be sure they are installed and installed correctly.

When any non-original-equipment wheel or lug nut/bolt is used on the vehicle, it is important that there is sufficient thread engagement between the lug nuts/bolts and the vehicle's hub. It's acceptable to increase the thread engagement by installing longer wheel studs in the hubs after verifying that the lug nuts don't bottom out on the studs. If the vehicle uses lug bolts, however, they must maintain as close to the original amount of thread engagement as possible. Longer lug bolts may cause interference with the parking brake or other components inside the hub.

Always torque the wheel's lug nuts/bolts to the hub using a "star" pattern (skipping a nut or so each time) until the vehicle's correct torque value is reached. Note: If you use

curbs, and unintentional trips through the run-off areas add their own unique extra stresses.

During track use, wheels will often reach temperatures never encountered on the street as they help dissipate brake heat. This constant cycling between the ambient temperature and the extremes encountered on the track can increase the fatigue rate of alloy wheels.

In normal street driving, wheels are typically removed from the vehicle only when the tires are being rotated (typically every 5,000 miles) or replaced (typically every 25,000 to 40,000 miles). But track wheels are typically removed from the vehicle at the start and finish of each race day, as well as anytime the vehicle's brakes or suspension are being serviced. Additionally, DOT-legal competition tires wear out and are replaced much more frequently than normal street tires. These extra tire mountings and vehicle installations can increase wheel fatigue as they wear out the

wheel's lug seats and the vehicle's lug nuts, studs, or hubs.

So what should track drivers do to take better care of their wheels and minimize the possibility of wheel failure?

Before going on the track, make certain that the wheel's installation

This is an extreme example of plus sizing. The wheel/tire on the right is the 16-inch diameter OE package on an Expedition. The wheel on the right is a 20-inch diameter Brevet wheel with a Toyo Proxes S/T tire. The diameter is very close to the same. A 22-inch wheel/tire could have been used.

wheel spacers that are thicker than the thickness of the hub, they also need to be wheel-and hubcentric to help distribute forces.

After coming off of the track each day, allow the wheels to cool, clean them front and back, and inspect for minute cracks, impact damage, and runout. At the first sign of a crack (regardless of size or location) or indication that the wheel has been bent, it should be removed from service and replaced with a good wheel.

Every time new tires are mounted, each wheel should be inspected to verify that it is round and true. If it is found to be bent, it should be removed from service and replaced with a good wheel.

If the wheel has been used for an extended period of time you may want to have a local machine shop professionally crack-test it in the off-season before considering subjecting it to another year of track use.

Wheels are a critical component to your car. Because they tend to fatigue slowly, periodic inspection will usually reveal the signs of aging and use (such as minute cracks in the wheels, spokes, or near the bolt holes) long before they can become a serious problem. If overlooked, however, a crack will concentrate the stresses in the weak area and spread until the wheel fails.

Before you buy your wheels, or hit the track, remember that track use and or other racing voids the manufacturers' warranties of all street wheels.

Tires

When it comes to tires, traction is increased when the tire rubber compound is softer and when the tire contact patch is bigger. The tread design and sidewall construction also play roles in allowing the tire contact patch to work on the road surface and maintain contact with the surface. Even the softest tire will not achieve good results if the tread design and sidewall construction miss the mark. Many factors

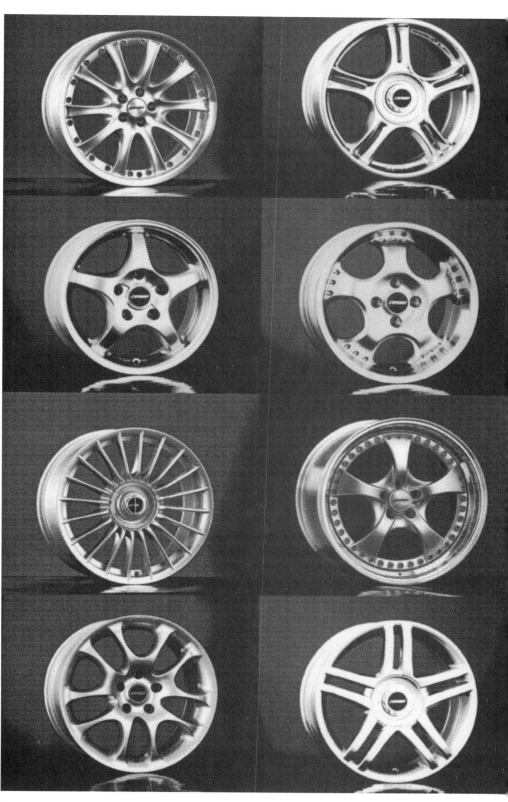

These wheels are all Zender alloys from Autotech Sport Tuning. The broad selection from most manufacturers allows a great deal of personalization. From the top left, the Authentic, the Challenge, the Champion, the Daytona, the Dynamic, the Impulse, the Le Mans, and the Winner.

This is a Zender Monza 18-x8.5-inch wheel used on our project Audi A4 Quattro Avant.

come into play when selecting tires for improved handling.

Performance versus Cost

Tires are not cheap, but dollar for dollar, they offer the single-biggest handling performance improvement. Performance tires cost less than high-performance tires, and ultra-high-performance tires cost the most. Race-compound tires actually cost slightly less outright, but even more important than outright expense is the cost per mile. Performance tires have softer rubber compounds than O.E. tires, meaning that they will wear out more quickly. Ultra-high-performance tires wear the quickest of the tires designed for highway driving. They also cost the most of the possible choices. Ultra-high-performance tires will last upward of 20,000 miles when driven hard or used for an occasional autocross or

track-day event. Better mileage is possible if you drive easier.

Grades of High-Performance Tires

There are great compromises available in most manufacturers' product lines in the high-performance arena that give good performance and excellent wear. But to really improve handling performance, the ultra-high-performance tires are in another world, one worth the expense if you really enjoy high-performance driving.

Plus Sizing

Plus sizing is a convenient way to categorize tires larger in wheel diameter and width for similar applications. When going up in tire size, or plus sizing, the wheel diameter increases as does the width. The width increase means a bigger tire contact patch on the road surface for improved traction. The wheel diameter increase is accommodated by a shorter sidewall height, keeping the diameter of the tire, or, more important, the rolling circumference of the tires, nearly equal to the original tire. This allows the suspension geometry, antilock brake sensors, gear ratio, and speedometer to function unaltered.

When plus sizing, it is both desirable and necessary to increase the section width (tread width) as well. It is desirable for the increase in contact patch area. It is necessary to maintain similar air volume within the tire when mounted on a wheel. Reducing the sidewall height while keeping the same outer diameter reduces the sidewall area. If the tread width remains stock, then the volume of air within the tire is reduced and the tire will not have the same characteristics as the original item. Increasing the tread width increases the area and compensates for the reduction of sidewall height. This allows the air volume to remain nearly the same as stock, which means the behavior over bumps, for example, is comparable to the stock. Although plus sizing provides a bigger contact patch, it also increases ride harshness.

This Lexus Grand-Am Cup street stock racecar uses Hoosier DOT-legal race compound tires for competition. Several companies offer street legal tires with race compounds for competition.

Tire and Wheel Sizing

It is important that the proper wheel width be used for a given tire size. Tire companies provide data for each tire they make, including wheel width recommendations. The range is usually about 2 inches in wheel width, with the middle width a good compromise for highway use. Using a rim outside the recommended range is very dangerous. If the rim is too narrow, the tire contact patch will crown and the sidewall beads will not seat properly. This could cause the tire to unseat from the wheel rim and deflate. At a minimum, this will ruin the tire and at worst, cause a crash. In performance applications, even the narrowest wheel width within recommendations may cause the tire to chatter or skip near the traction limit.

Putting a tire on a rim that is too wide, beyond width recommendations, is also a mistake. The tire will not seat properly on the rim bead and may not even inflate.

Within the range of recommended wheel widths for a specific tire, the wider wheel choice is best. When a tire is on the widest recommended wheel, the tire contact patch is the most equally loaded because it receives the greatest base of support from the rim. For a specific competition class where wheel width is limited, using a tire with a smaller cross-section width is often better than trying to use the widest tire that will fit in the fender well on a rim that is narrower than optimum.

Tire Clearance

A lack of tire clearance is both costly and dangerous. A rubbing tire can wear through and blow out. At a minimum, tire wear is accelerated. Most tire shops specializing in ultra-high-performance tires know how to properly fit wheel/tire combinations for specific applications. Many tire and wheel manufacturers, along with some retailers and mail order dealers, have Web sites with fitment guides

This tire cutaway shows the layers of belts that make up an ultra-high-performance tire. *Tire Rack*

that will tell you what will work for your specific vehicle.

Ride and Performance Considerations

Ultra-high-performance tires are more responsive and provide improved grip. One of the ways they accomplish this is by using stiffer sidewall construction. Additionally, plus sizing means shorter sidewalls, which further increase tire sidewall stiffness. This translates into increased ride harshness because there's less tire sidewall to absorb bumps.

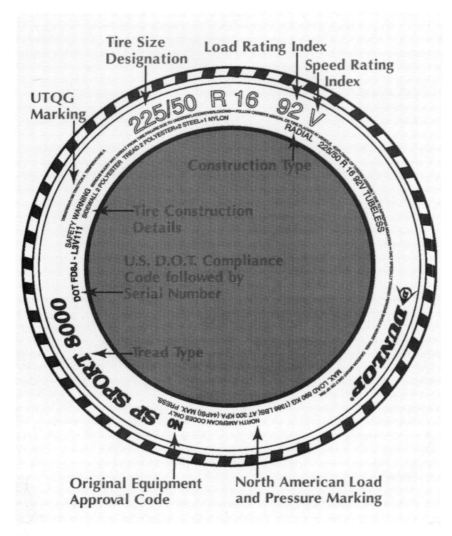

Tire Size Designation

Load Rating Index

Speed Rating Index

UTQG Marking

225/50 R 16 92 V

Construction Type

Tire Construction Details

U.S. D.O.T. Compliance Code followed by Serial Number

Tread Type

Original Equipment Approval Code

North American Load and Pressure Marking

This diagram explains terminology on the tire sidewall. *Tire Rack*

The trade-off is more traction and especially better responsiveness versus ride-quality degradation. Add stiffer suspension components and less suspension bump travel and the ride can become downright stiff, even uncomfortable. An aggressive package can mean some level of discomfort on bumpy roads, so carefully consider your priorities before taking the plunge.

Race-Compound DOT Tires

Race-compound DOT street-legal tires make gobs of traction—in the dry! In the wet, forget it. You may as well have bald tires on ice. They also wear quickly, with a useful life of about 10,000 miles of normal street and highway driving, though I've never met anyone driving on race-compound DOT tires who drives normally. Between the wear and the poor wet traction, these tires are best left to track days, autocrossing, and racing. If you have a dual-purpose vehicle, save your race-compound tires for the track itself and get there on a high-or ultra-high-performance tire.

Wet versus Dry Traction

Most original-equipment tires have a compromise design, allowing good traction in both wet and dry conditions. These tires have tread patterns that work well in the wet but reduce steering responsiveness in dry

The plus concept of sizing allows a wider, more aggressive tire on a larger diameter wheel without changing the tire diameter so that antilock brake systems and speedometers are not affected. *Tire Rack*

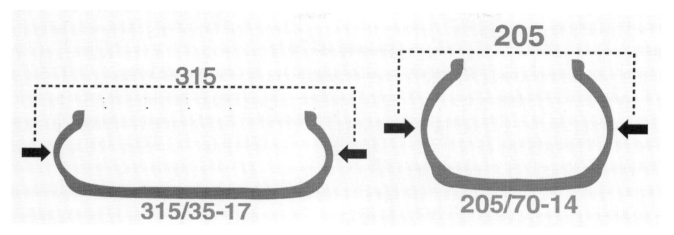

This illustration shows the relative differences in width and sidewall section height of a 205/70-14 tire and a 315/35-17 tire. *Tire Rack*

situations. High- and ultra-high-performance tires have softer tread compounds and much more aggressive tread patterns, which usually means a lower void ratio (the area of the grooves at the tire contact patch versus the area of rubber at the patch). Higher void ratios mean more resistance to hydroplaning but less rubber on the ground. Lower void ratios increase traction but offer less resistance to hydroplaning. Original-equipment tires have higher void ratios, while performance, high-performance, and ultra-high-performance tires have smaller and smaller void ratios.

Wet traction is influenced by the tread compound as well. Ultra-high-performance tires with higher amounts of silica compound provide better grip in wet conditions. This usually reduces dry traction slightly, but if you live in a rainy environment, the trade-off can be a good one.

Wider tires are also less resistant to hydroplaning. More rubber on the road, whether from greater section width or lower void ratio, means more hydroplaning. Additionally, wider tires do not track as well over longitudinal grooves, expansion strips, and road repairs. While this is mostly an annoyance in the dry, it can be very edgy in wet weather. If you live in a rainy area, or have a severe rainy season, have a second set of tires for bad weather. And

The ultra-high-performance tire on the left has a tread design radically different from the snow tire on the right. The void ratios are very different with the snow tire having a much higher void ratio, meaning that the tread has more groove area. The ultra-high-performance tire has much greater dry grip, but the snow tire is superior on any slippery surface.

In slippery winter conditions, snow tires like the Toyo Observe on our project Audi A4 Avant Quattro provide exceptional grip. While snow tires are much better on ice than all but studded tires, nothing has very good grip on ice.

This is plus sizing to the extreme. The Toyo Proxes S/T is a 20-inch tire compared to the stock tire from a Ford Expedition. The S/T offers far more grip for cornering and braking with only a small increase in ride harshness.

if you live in a snowy climate, mud and snow tires are the only way to go for the best grip possible.

Tire Care

Tires are very durable, but there are several items to be aware of to get the most wear, reliability, and safety from them.

• Keep your tires at the proper
    inflation pressure at all times.
• Avoid hitting curbs.
• Check sidewalls for damage
    regularly.

If you have a second set of tires for track days, autocrossing, wet weather, or winter driving, put the set off the car in green or black plastic trash bags for storage. This reduces the weathering effects and helps keep the tires more supple. It prevents the tread compound from hardening as quickly over time.

Tire Feel and Drivability

Every tire has a personality of its own. And some drivers prefer certain

Three widely varying tread pattern designs on DOT legal race compound tires. On the left is the Yokohama Advan A032R with the curved grooves. In the middle is the Kumho Victoracer 700. On the right is the Toyo Proxes RA-1. All three are comparable in performance and wear when the car is tuned to work with the specific characteristics of each tire.

characteristics in a tire. While the grip of a tire comes from the tread compound and design, the personality lives in the sidewall construction. Some tires are instantly responsive to steering inputs. They provide solid feedback through the controls and the seat of the driver's pants. They are predictable and make it easy to be smooth and consistent at the wheel.

On the other hand, some tires feel like rubber bands, constantly expand-

ing and contracting. Just about the time you think the tire is going to stabilize, it feels like the sidewall springs back and the handling balance is totally altered. It's hard to drive fast consistently on tires like that, and they certainly do not instill confidence.

A fairly stiff tire sidewall that is linear in its response to steering inputs and a good tread pattern design make for a tire that is both

predictable and stable in feel. These tires can be a joy to drive on. The tire evaluation sidebars in this chapter cover all tires that I have extensive experience with in testing or on the track. The evaluations are my opinion and other tires not listed may be as good or better. Every driver prefers a different feel in a tire, so understand that my preferences may be different from yours.

TOYO TIRES

The Toyo Proxes T1S ultra-high-performance tire. *Toyo Tire USA*

Traction is the key success in any type of motorsport and tires are the key to traction. I first raced on Toyo Tires in 1972 when the SCCA introduced the Showroom Stock class. I also had an opportunity to test the first of the Proxes line about eight years ago, but this was the first time I drove on the race compound Proxes and the street T1 Plus.

The grip of the Toyos—both models—is outstanding. But just as important, both the RA-1 and the T1 Plus tires are totally predictable and responsive to driver inputs. Even though the RA-1 is a 15-inch tire and the T1 plus is a 17-inch tire, you can't tell any difference in the balance and response between the tires. The RA-1's have more grip, but the feel is virtually identical. This is due to the sidewall construction of the tire providing the same dynamic response and feel. Since the tires are very easy to drive to the limits of traction, Toyo has a real winner with these tires.

On the grip side, the RA-1 compound is excellent, but the T1 Plus is a surprise, offering as much or more grip than some older race-compound DOT tires. For a street tire offering good wear characteristics, the T1 Plus is hard to beat. The RA-1 has been proven in racing over and over. They offer exceptional grip over the full life of the tread, unlike many tires that fall off as the tread wears and the tires are heat cycled. The Toyos seem to keep going and going until the tread is worn away. That makes the RA-1 not only a top performer but also a cost-effective competition tire.

We also tested a set of Proxes S/T tires on our Expedition project SUV, and the difference in grip is amazing. With no other modifications to the SUV, braking and cornering performance are much better. And the Observe snow tires on the Audi project car also provide amazing traction on snowy and wet roads. The increase in traction instills confidence and improves safety, which makes the entire snow-driving experience great fun.

The Toyo Proxes RA-1 street legal, race compound competition tire. *Toyo Tire USA*

The Toyo Proxes S/T high-performance truck and SUV tire. *Toyo Tire USA*

The Toyo Observe Mud and Snow tire.

YOKOHAMA TIRES

Over the years I have tested and raced on several types of Yokohama tires. In all cases, they have been excellent. Their ultra-high-performance and high-performance tires offer excellent grip, good wear, and very predicable responses to driver control inputs. A tire with no surprises or quirky behavior is always welcomed at the limits of traction, and Yokohama tires have been great fun to drive on. The Yokohama street legal race compound competition tires, like the AO32R, are also superb tires. They offer excellent traction combined with very good wear. The tires can take considerable abuse and keep on going. Additionally, the level of traction after the first session on the tires stays at a very high level throughout the entire tread life of the tire. For any application, Yokohama tires provide an excellent choice.

The Yokohama AVS Sport ultra-high-performance tire. *Yokohama Tire*

The Yokohama AVS S4 is an all-season ultra-high-performance tire offering slightly less dry grip but better wet traction than the Parada. *Yokohama Tire*

The Yokohama A032R is a street legal race compound competition tire offering great grip and good wear characteristics for its type. *Yokohama Tire*

The Yokohama Parada ultra-high-performance tire offers slightly less grip but better wear than the AVS Sport. *Yokohama Tire*

CONTINENTAL

The Continental ContiSport Contact ultra-high-performance tire was my first experience on Continentals. I was very pleasantly surprised by the performance. We tried a set of 215/40-17 Contacts as plus two tires on our project Accord. These tires offer really good grip, nearly as good as some of the pricier ultra-high-performance tires I've tried. While grip is slightly less, wear is considerably better and road noise from the tread pattern and compound is much less than many comparable tires. If you drive your car daily on long commutes, road noise and wear become major factors. The ContiSport Contact is a great compromise.

The Continental ContiSport Contact ultra-high-performance tire offers great grip with good wear and a relatively quite ride.

BFGoodrich

The g-Force T/A KD is an exceptional ultra-high-performance tire offering high levels of traction and responsiveness with good wear characteristics.

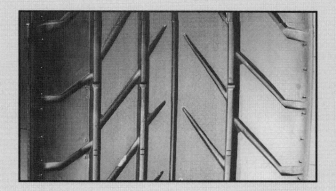

The BFG Scorcher T/A is a high-performance tire available in three colors of tread stripes including yellow, blue, and red. *BFGoodrich Tires*

HOOSIER

Hoosier is well-known as a racing tire manufacturer. It is no surprise that their DOT-legal race compound tires are the fastest in most applications. These are excellent tires and some sizes are available in a softer compound for autocrossing. But performance comes at a price, and the Hoosiers typically cost a little more than other DOT legal race compound tires. They also wear faster.

The Hoosier Sports Car is a street legal race compound competition tire. This tire has the softest compound of current street legal competition tires, so it is faster initially, but tends to lose some grip over time and wears more quickly than other street-legal race compound tires. *Hoosier Tire*

KUMHO

Kumho is fairly new to the U.S. performance tire market, but the company has gained considerable attention in the last couple of years. After testing its Ecsta Supra 712 ultra-high-performance tire and the V700 Victoracer DOT competition tire, we understood the attention. The tires work and they are very reasonably priced.

We tried a set of 205/55R15 Ecsta Supra 712 tires on the Honda Accord project using the stock rims. This tire is just a bit narrower than the Continental ContiSport tire, but the grip is just as good. The slightly more aggressive tread pattern on the Ecsta Supra 712 makes just a little more noise on the highway, but the 15-inch rim versus the 17-inchers makes for a more comfortable ride. The flip side of the 15-inch rims is a slightly slower response to steering inputs, but this would only have an effect on a straight-line slalom course, not at the limits of traction in a normal cornering situation.

The V700 Victoracer DOT competition tire also lives up to its reputation. This tire works as well as other DOT race compound tires, is easy to drive with no surprises, and it responds well to tuning. We did not get enough laps to determine wear with accuracy, but early signs indicate good wear on par with similar Yokohama and Toyo DOT race tires. This tire would be well worth trying for track days, autocrossing, or club level road racing.

This is the tread pattern of the Kumho Ecsta Supra 712 ultra-high-performance tire.

A 205/55 R15 Kumho Ecsta Supra 712 ultra-high-performance tire mounted on our project Accord's stock wheels.

GENERAL

More than a decade ago, I raced on General Tires in the International Sedan series and was pleasantly surprised by the level of performance. General was new to DOT race tires during that period, but after some chassis tuning, the tires worked just as well as the other race compound DOT tires we tried. Today General offers a range of high-performance all-season tires for cars and trucks. We tested a set of the General Grabber AW tires on our project Ford Expedition. These tires are original equipment tires on many SUVs and light trucks, including 1999 and newer Expeditions. Ford clearly made a good choice going to the General Grabbers compared to the 1997 OE tires. The generals are much better with more grip, equal ride quality, and less road noise. Add the all-season performance and the driving conditions that the Expedition is used in and the Grabber is a perfect choice.

 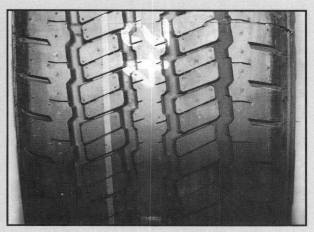

The General Grabber AW is used on many SUVs and light trucks as original equipment and is an excellent OE replacement tire for these vehicles. The traction is excellent and the all-season design performs well in all road conditions just short of ice.

Chapter Eight
Brakes

The only thing worse than brakes that won't stop is a steering wheel that won't steer. Brakes are a crucial system on any car, and even more important for a high-performance or competition vehicle. The good news is that most stock brake systems work extremely well in most highway driving conditions. But poor maintenance can ruin the effectiveness of a brake system quickly. Brake upgrades can improve performance significantly as long as the system is well-engineered or the individual components are compatible with the remaining stock parts.

For motorsports, different forms of competition have specific brake system requirements. Some are compatible with highway driving and some are not. In this chapter we will explore various brake system components, what they do, and how they fit specific applications and needs.

Brake Kits

Brake kits are at the top of the brake system–improvement food chain. Larger calipers, rotors, mounting hardware, and job-specific brake pads are the minimum components in a brake system upgrade. Steel braided brake lines, uprated master cylinders, and proportioning valves/bias adjusters may also be included in a package. If you want or need to upgrade your brake system with a complete package, there are several key points to keep in mind. First, the system must be the right one for your application: street, mountain roads, autocrossing, rallying, track days, or road racing. A less expensive upgrade intended for high-performance street applications will be susceptible to premature wear or failure from sustained use on the track. Don't skimp on stopping power.

Brakes are a critical system for performance and safety. This British Touring Car has massive brakes, but performance is hurt when a single wheel locks up as shown on the left rear of the car.

The second thing to keep in mind is that the system must be compatible with your vehicle. Do the calipers bolt on or are mounting brackets provided? Are the rotors compatible with the stock spindles and wheel bearings? If not, are the necessary components part of the package? Are the hydraulic fittings and threads compatible with your vehicle? If not, are adapters provided?

Third, is the system properly engineered for your vehicle? The key issue here, beyond the fitment issues discussed above, is the hydraulic system design. For the proper pedal feel and performance, the master cylinders must be compatible with the piston area of the calipers. If they are not compatible, the brakes will require too much pedal pressure or will lack adequate clamping force to brake at the limits of traction, or there will be inadequate pedal travel to brake smoothly (the brakes are touchy and too sensitive to small pedal applications). None of these situations are acceptable, so finding a well-engineered system is critical. Many companies such as those mentioned in this chapter work diligently to engineer effective brake systems. Brake systems are a major investment. If you are uncertain about the system for your vehicle from a specific manufacturer, ask for a reference from a customer with the same vehicle.

Next, you need to know the wheel size and inside rim clearance needed for the new calipers and rotors. Your current wheels may be too small to house the new parts.

Finally, if your vehicle is intended for competition, make sure that brake upgrades are allowed in the class you intend to compete in.

Brake Pads

The easiest and least expensive brake upgrade is brake pads. Braking performance can be greatly enhanced with the proper high-performance set of brake pads. The most important

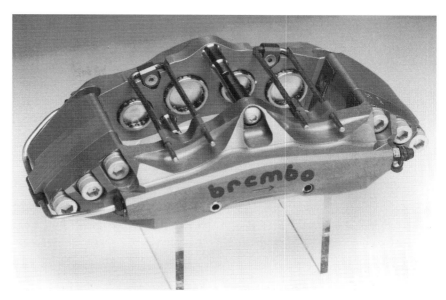

Large, multipiston calipers like this eight-piston Brembo caliper provide great amounts of stopping power for performance applications. Note the variation in piston diameters. This helps equalize pressure against the brake pad and helps to keep pad wear even front to rear. *Brembo USA*

This Wilwood rotor, caliper, and hat will improve braking performance on Hondas and Acuras considerably. *Wilwood*

Brembo makes a wide range of high-performance brake kits for many applications. A well-engineered kit reduces potential fitment problems and ensures maximum performance. This kit includes rotors, calipers, and caliper-mounting adapters, hardware, and steel braided brake lines. *Brembo USA*

the limit of traction. Brake fade is almost not an issue with hard brake pads, but is potentially a real problem with soft pad compounds.

For such motorsports activities as autocrossing, where brakes are used very hard but for only about one minute or less at a time, or rallying, where the traction is low so brake forces are less, medium-hard compounds work well. Other applications, such as drag racing where top speed and vehicle weight are critical factors, require different brake pad compounds. In all cases, consult with the manufacturer to determine the correct pad for your vehicle and the best compound for your application.

Brake Rotors

Another simple and relatively inexpensive brake upgrade is the brake rotor. Several companies make original-equipment replacement rotors that are superior to the stock rotors, and in some cases, cheaper than factory replacement parts. Most cars today come with vented front and solid rear rotors. Aftermarket replacement rotors should be of the same configuration, diameter, and thickness as the stock rotors. This ensures compatibility with the stock calipers. Any change in

criterion for pads is the intended application. Most companies offer a variety of brake pad compounds for different uses. For street and highway, where you can drive many miles without a brake application, or may need to make a panic stop at any time, brake pad compounds need to be relatively soft so that maximum braking efficiency is at hand instantly. Harder compounds have higher operating temperatures for

maximum braking force and require longer to warm up. The first hard stop you make on cold brakes could take as much as 25 percent more distance—not a good thing in a panic stop situation.

But the hard compound pads would be ideal for road racing situations where full-force brake applications occur several times a minute, and pad overheating could hurt performance greatly after a few applications at

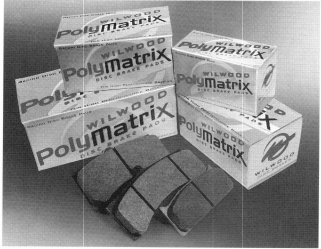

Brake pads play a key role in performance. Different applications require different compounds. Autocrossing has different needs from road racing, which is different from rallying or street driving. Consult with a pad manufacturer for the right pad for a given application. *Wilwood*

diameter or thickness would require new calipers. Many aftermarket front rotors come with new wheel bearings when the hub is part of the rotor. The wheel bearings and seals should be replaced if they are not included with the rotors. The biggest gains come from front rotor replacement with smaller gains from the rear, especially on front-drive cars.

Brake Calipers

If you want to upgrade calipers, you'll need a complete kit, including new rotors. Most often stock calipers are single-piston designs with the outside half of the caliper on pins that allow it to slide. With this design, all of the braking force is applied from one side with the piston pushing the inside and pulling the outside pad. Some designs use two pistons with a single piston on each side. Both pads are pushed directly by pistons, making this design more efficient. Most high-end and aftermarket brake kits feature four-, six-, or eight-piston calipers with multiple pistons on each side of the caliper. These designs allow greater efficiency by applying force over a larger area, which also allows better cooling and heat dissipation. Some designs use larger pistons on the leading edge of the caliper so more force is applied to the leading edge of the pad and rotor. This improves the smoothness of brake applications, reduces brake noise, and improves pad life.

Brake Lines

Stock rubber brake hoses expand when the pedal is pushed, and that takes more pedal travel and reduces positive feedback to the driver. Steel braided lines eliminate the expansion, reducing pedal travel and increasing positive feedback from the tire contact patches.

Brake Fluid

Brake fluid should be changed routinely in any high-performance application, especially in motorsports use. Brake fluid is hygroscopic, meaning

Excessive heat buildup can cause a brake rotor to crack. This rotor is now useless, except for scrap.

Drilled rotors allow the gas created by hot brake pads under severe conditions to escape. The gas buildup between the rotor and the pad is one cause of brake fade. Cross-drilled rotors reduce brake fade.

Steel-braided brake lines reduce flex compared to rubber hoses. This improves responsiveness and pedal feel and adds an extra margin of safety.

fluids that are designed for high-performance and motorsports applications.

Master Cylinders

Most stock master cylinders are adequate for high-performance applications and even club-level racing and rallying when used with stock calipers. With aftermarket calipers, either the calipers must be engineered to work with stock master cylinders so that pedal feel, travel, and pedal pressure remain near stock, or new master cylinders should be part of the coordinated brake package.

The engineering side of this is complex. If the master cylinders are not properly mated to the calipers, the braking effort could change, requiring considerable effort by the driver to brake. Additionally, the pedal travel could become too much for effective braking, or be inadequate to fully utilize the brakes up to the limits of tire traction. Finally, the braking pressure from front to rear can change with a caliper change. This means that either the front or rear brakes could lock up too early for effective stopping, yielding excessive tire wear and, worse, much longer stopping distances.

The master cylinders must be compatible with the calipers to ensure the optimum function of the brake system. This transcends performance and becomes a safety issue, so make sure any brake system changes will not compromise safety and performance.

Consult with the brake manufacturers about these issues. Then test the new system under safe and forgiving conditions to ensure that everything is working properly with the system.

Proportioning Valves

A proportioning valve reduces hydraulic line pressure between the brake master cylinder and the caliper pistons at one end, front or rear, where there is a dual master cylinder system. The valves are adjustable, allowing the fine-tuning of brake line pressure to one end of the car.

it absorbs water vapor from the atmosphere. Water in the brake fluid reduces the boiling point of the fluid and can cause severe brake fade. Bleeding the brakes regularly, say every time you change the oil, will keep fresh brake fluid in the system and ensure that you have a brake system that will operate to its peak potential at all times.

Because of the hygroscopic nature of brake fluid, use only small pint bottles

and keep the bottle closed at all times when not actually pouring fluid into the master cylinder reservoir. Also, keep the cap on the master cylinder reservoir at all times when not adding brake fluid. Use only DOT 4 or better brake fluid. Synthetic fluids are compressible and have lower boiling points so they are not recommended. Several companies, including brake manufacturers, market high-temperature brake

Above and above right: Brake fluid must be high temperature for performance applications. Never use less than a DOT 3-grade fluid for stock brakes. Use high-temperature brake fluids if upgrading any part of the brake system including brake pads. Brake fluid absorbs moisture from the atmosphere. That reduces the boiling point and leads to brake fade and a spongy pedal when brakes get hot. Use small cans of fluid and keep them closed unless pouring. Bleed the system often, especially for any motorsports applications. *Wilwood*

Proportioning valves are usually, but not always, used on the rear brakes. The valve should be plumbed into the system where wheel lock-up occurs first. In this way, line pressure can be reduced so that the front tires lock up just before the rear tires. This improves stability and ensures that the vehicle is able to brake at the absolute limits of tire traction. Of course, with antilock brakes at each wheel, lock-up will not occur. The antilock brake system is like an electronically controlled proportioning valve at each wheel.

Brake Bias

Brake bias is the balance between the front and rear brake line pressure. When a brake system is engineered, the goal is to get all four tires locking at

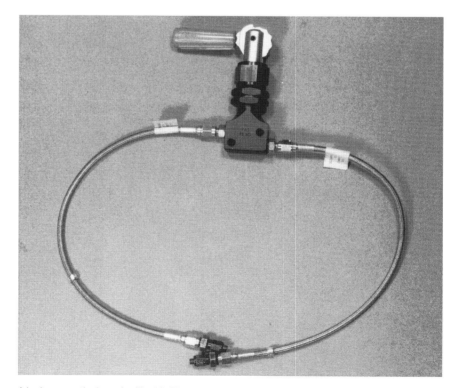

A brake proportioning valve like this Tilton unit allows easy adjustment of front to rear brake bias. Fine tuning brake bias allows front and rear wheel lockup to occur at the same time, improving braking performance.

the same time, with the fronts locking just before the rears for stability. Many racecars have a brake bias adjustment, some adjustable in the cockpit, that allows fine-tuning of the brake balance front to rear.

Unlike a brake proportioning valve, which alters hydraulic pressure, the bias adjuster alters the mechanical advantage between the front and rear master cylinders between the pedal and the master cylinder actuating rods. The effect is the same as a proportioning valve, but the means is different. Most often the bias adjuster is part of a complete pedal assembly, including the dual master cylinders. It is unusual for a bias adjuster to be an add-on part for existing master cylinders. Many racecars equipped with aftermarket pedal assemblies with master cylinders and bias adjusters also use a proportioning valve to fine-tune brake balance as track conditions and fuel loads change.

Cooling

If you experience brake fade during the type of driving you do, then brake cooling is an issue. Most common in road racing and track-day events, brake fade can also occur when driving in the mountains and canyons, where braking forces exceed normal driving conditions. Brake fade can be caused by boiling brake fluid or overheated brake pads. The first solution for brake fade is to use the best, highest-boiling-point brake fluid available, and bleed the brakes routinely. The second solution is to use the right brake pad compound for your vehicle and application. But even if brake fade is not an issue, cooling the brakes, especially in a competition situation, will improve pad and rotor life and overall braking efficiency.

Brake cooling is especially important at the front, where most of the braking force occurs. There are several ways to duct air to the brake rotors, but the best is the use of an NACA duct or a duct in the air dam or front spoiler. (See the accompanying photos.) The ducted air should flow to the center of the rotor on a vented rotor, not the braking surface of the rotor. This cools the rotor more effectively and evenly.

If you compete with your car, especially on a road course, and the brakes are really hot at the end of a session, be sure to release the brake pedal as soon as possible in the pit area. Also, move the car a foot or two every minute or so to ensure that heat sinking does not occur where the pads are in contact with the rotors. This will keep rotors from warping and increase brake pad and rotor life.

Brake Pad and Rotor Bedding

New brake rotors and pads need to be bedded in for maximum braking efficiency. Bedding is equally important for street performance as it is for race track performance. As smooth as new brake rotors are, there are still imperfections in the surface, and the pads need to be perfectly mated to the rotor. This is especially true with new brake pads on old rotors. New rotors should never be used with old brake pads. The pads are softer, but old pads on new rotors will never properly bed in and braking effectiveness will never be at the optimum.

Additionally, new brake pads use a bonding agent to hold the particles comprising the pad material together. The bonding agent vaporizes with high temperatures, creating a gas that flows between the pad and rotor surfaces.

Keeping brakes cool is critical for brake performance in high speed and continued use applications. Ducting cool air to the brakes helps cool the rotor and fluid. Air should be fed into the center of the rotor if the rotor has a vane. This allows cooling from the inside out and is easier and more effective for the brakes. Ducting can be simple or complicated.

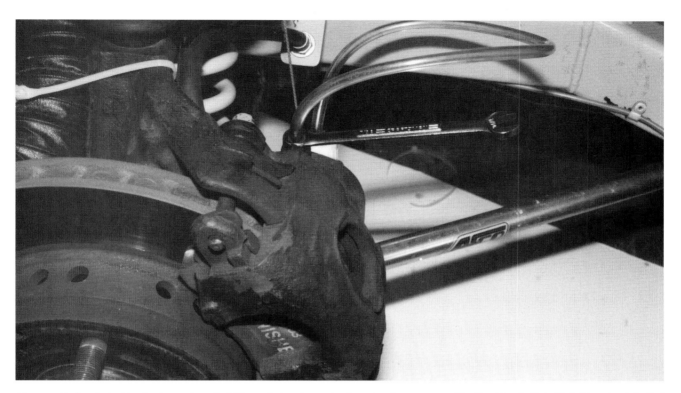

Above and below: Brake bleeding is very important. These photos show a simple system for one-person bleeding. The plastic bottle holds a clear tube that attaches to the caliper bleed fitting. Some brake fluid in the bottom of the bottle covering the end of the tube will keep air from being sucked into the system as the brake pedal is depressed with the bleed valve open. This forces air out of the system without the need for maintaining pedal pressure while the valve is open. Gravity will help the process. Start with the caliper the greatest distance away from the master cylinder and add fluid to the master cylinder often.

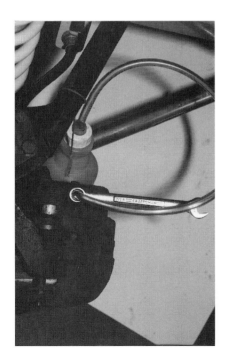

This causes a type of brake fade called "green fade." The only way to eliminate this is to bed the brake pads properly so that the bonding agent is eliminated just below the surface.

Both new rotors and new pads are bedded the same way. When brand new, the pads and rotors need to be heated by hard brake applications to a high temperature, then cooled to ambient temperature before being used again. This causes the pad and rotor surfaces to mate perfectly and reduces the bonding agent at the surface of the pad material, also eliminating green fade. To do this, make several stops (or speed reductions on a race track) from speed, then let the brakes cool completely. Now the brakes are bedded and will provide maximum stopping efficiency throughout their life. Some manufacturers provide a bedding service for pads and rotors for an additional charge.

Brake Noise

Brake noise or squeal can be caused by excessive heat, improper bedding, or too much pressure applied to the trailing edge of the pad by the brake caliper pistons. Brake noise is an indication of a problem, with three possible solutions. If the noise occurs only when the brakes are very hot, brake cooling or a different pad compound would be in order. If the pads were not bedded properly, or at all, the only solution is to use new brake pads and bed them properly before extended hard use. If these possibilities are not the problem, there is likely too much piston pressure on the trailing edge of the brake pad. Some calipers are designed with larger pistons on the leading edge to eliminate this problem. If the calipers are stock, try installing a new set of pads that are ground at a slight angle on the surface to eliminate the squeal problem.

Chapter Nine
Aerodynamics

This Stillen Aero kit creates a radical change to the styling of the Honda Civic. This kit improves internal aerodynamics and cooling as well. *Stillen*

Aerodynamics plays a role in performance by affecting drag and downforce. Drag affects top speed and, to a small degree, acceleration. Downforce increases traction for braking, cornering, and acceleration off the corners. Increasing downforce is an important part of aerodynamic engineering. The trick is finding the best balance between drag reduction and downforce. These two factors are not compatible, so aero kit manufacturers and race teams must compromise to create an effective package.

On the highway, while aerodynamic drag is always a factor, it is not a major one. And downforce, even with highly efficient aero packaging, is so small that it isn't really an important consideration. At highway speeds, not enough downforce is created to really matter from a traction perspective. There are two factors to consider when looking at aerodynamics relative to on-track performance. Drag, or the force caused by wind resistance, slows the car. Downforce, or negative lift, affects tire traction. Let's look at drag first.

Aerodynamic Drag

The easiest way to experience aerodynamic drag is to put your hand out the window of a car moving at 60 miles per hour. Hold your palm forward and feel the wind pressure pushing your hand back. At 60 miles per hour, the wind force makes it difficult to hold your hand steady.

The force against your hand is aerodynamic drag. It is proportional to the area of your hand. If you put on a glove that makes your hand twice as big, the force will be two times more.

Aero kits add greatly to the look of a car. Many aero kits on the street have little influence on handling since they provide little downforce and usually increase aerodynamic drag considerably.

Rotate your hand so that the area at a right angle to the direction of airflow is one half the size and the force against your hand is half as much. The area facing the airflow is called frontal area, and the amount of drag is proportional to the frontal area. Obviously, reducing frontal area as much as possible reduces aerodynamic drag and improves performance on the track.

The speed at which the car is moving through the air also affects the amount of aerodynamic drag. This is a much bigger factor, however. If you double the speed, the aerodynamic drag force is four times greater. Put your hand back out the window at 60 miles per hour. Let's say the force pushing against your hand is 25 pounds per square inch at that speed. If we double the speed to 120 miles per hour, the force will quadruple to 100 pounds per square inch. If we cut the speed to 30 miles per hour, the force is reduced to only 6.25 psi.

One way to reduce aerodynamic drag on a racecar is to slow down—not a very good option. It takes about 115 horsepower to overcome aerodynamic drag on a Winston Cup car at 100 miles per hour. To go 200 miles per hour requires four times more power, or about 460 horsepower. That's about the power a restrictor-plate engine produces. Without a restrictor plate, a Winston Cup car would have a top speed of about 250 miles per hour, which

would mean a lap speed at Daytona of around 220 to 225 miles per hour.

Finally, the shape of the body affects aerodynamic drag forces. If you rotate your hand in the air stream you are reducing frontal area, but you also change the shape of your hand. The more "slippery" shape also reduces drag. A given shape of an object will have a specific effect on airflow over that shape. This is called the drag coefficient. The drag coefficient times the frontal area gives the relative amount of aerodynamic drag at a given speed. A larger drag coefficient means more aerodynamic drag. Most of the aerodynamics work done by race teams and

auto makers focuses on reducing aerodynamic drag coefficients.

A flat plate headed directly into the air stream has a drag coefficient of almost 1.2. A smooth ball has a drag coefficient of 0.47. A streamlined body, like a symmetrical airplane wing, in the air stream, has a drag coefficient of 0.04, about as low as possible. Given equal frontal area, if your open hand against the windflow created 25 pounds of drag force, then the streamlined shape of the same frontal area would create only 1 pound of force. That's a huge difference.

What's interesting is if we take that streamlined shape, cut it in half,

Aerodynamics play a major role in handling performance, especially at high speed.

Rear spoilers and wings come in several varieties and have varying effects on drag and downforce. Each of these designs is effective. In motorsports, rules usually dictate what you can run aerodynamically.

and put it on the ground, the drag coefficient more than doubles to 0.09. The ground has a big effect on drag, always increasing it. Pilots know about this effect, called the ground effect, when landing a plane. Rotating wheels also increase the drag coefficient. With significant effort, the drag coefficient on a Winston Cup car has been cut to about 0.28 to 0.29, a fairly small number, and lower than the drag coefficient on an Indy car or Grand Prix car.

Aerodynamics and Car Performance

Two key factors affect car performance aerodynamically. Drag reduces top speed for a given horsepower and also reduces acceleration. Total downforce, or lift, affects traction. Any positive lift reduces traction. Downforce, or negative lift, increases load on the tires and therefore increases traction. But more downforce means more drag. Compromise is everything. The better the compromise, the better the on-track performance. The compromise is called the lift/drag ratio: how much lift (or downforce) is present for a given amount of drag. This can be measured in a wind tunnel or during testing. But for the highway, aerodynamics is effectively engineered by the auto manufacturers. Aero kits are popular additions for performance vehicles, so let's look at street packages first, then the aerodynamic needs for motorsports.

Aero Kits

Aero kits can look really cool, which is the only justification for adding one to your street performance car. If performance gains are your only goal for the street, then aero kits are at best a wash. A car lowered with suspension modifications will reduce drag by reducing frontal area and underbody turbulence. An aero kit at best will reduce air under the car and reduce drag. But most aero kits add frontal area, and that increases aero drag. Most kits do little to reduce drag coefficients. Some aero kits increase downforce slightly, but at highway speeds the effect is small. And the weight of the kit will also adversely affect acceleration. In all cases, the effects on fuel consumption are minimal in either direction. If you want the look, go for it. Otherwise, put the money elsewhere.

Motorsports

The goal of motorsports is to improve performance. In most cases with most vehicles on most tracks, reducing drag is important, but increasing downforce is more important. On very fast road courses reducing drag may be a higher priority, but for stock-bodied vehicles that would be unusual. Aero kits are rarely allowed for most cars in most motorsports classes. If they are, seeing test results on lift/drag ratios will tell you if they may be beneficial. If there are no test results, then the kit is probably ineffective for competition; otherwise the manufacturer would have tested the kit and would tout its benefits.

What is usually allowed for competition is a front air dam or splitter and a rear spoiler or wing. Let's look at each of these individually.

Air Dams

An air dam is an aero device mounted vertically below the front bumper, usually following the contour of the bumper. It is mounted as close to the ground as possible, or as close as the rules allow. Air dams work by minimizing airflow under the car. This reduces drag (underbody turbulence) and creates downforce by creating a partial vacuum under the car.

The air dam itself is not an aerodynamically sound shape and creates no downforce on its own. Vertical, or near vertical, air dams work the best. Production cars adding air dams—but without a rear spoiler or wing—often experience oversteer in high-speed corners when the car previously was well balanced in the same turns. The front downforce is making the front tires stick more, so cornering speeds go up until the rear tires run out of traction. If you find that is a problem, work on getting some rear downforce.

Inclined front spoilers, looking like a cow catcher on a steam locomotive, may look like they create some downforce, but they do not. They increase drag but make no downforce. A wing shape is needed to create downforce. With an inclined spoiler, air gets trapped underneath, causing turbulence and possibly some lift.

Splitters

A splitter is an air dam with a horizontal, rounded forward extension at the bottom of the dam. These extensions are often adjustable to alter the amount of downforce. They create downforce through air pressure on the leading edge of the extension, which acts like a lever. The longer the lever, the more the downforce. But if the lever is too long, flow separation reduces pressure and downforce. In addition to increased downforce, the splitter allows adjustments to fine-tune handling balance for high-speed turns. Most cars with efficient rear airfoil-shaped wings need a splitter to maintain aerodynamic downforce balance.

Rear Spoilers

A rear spoiler is usually a flat plate attached to the rear deck lid mounted at an angle. The spoiler is designed to alter airflow to create some downforce, or reduce lift. The height of the spoiler is usually dictated by rules, but if not, one too tall creates too much drag without a significant increase in downforce. The angle of the spoiler is also important. If the angle is too steep, flow separation occurs and creates turbulence and increases drag. If the angle is too shallow, little or no downforce will be created. Spoilers and air dams are easily fabricated from 1/8 inch to 3/16 inch thick aluminum sheet. The angle can be adjusted by bending the spoiler material to a greater or lesser degree.

Wings

Wings are the most efficient of all aero devices, but to work effectively, they must be designed according to a NACA or similar wing profile. These shapes create the most lift (downforce, in our case) and the least drag, both desirable for on-track performance. Wings are most effective when the aspect ratio is high. The aspect ratio is the width divided by the chord length (the distance between the leading and trailing edges of the airfoil). A wide wing with a short chord has a better lift/drag ratio, increasing downforce more than drag. The angle of attack of a wing, or the angle from horizontal relative to the direction of airflow, is also critical. If the angle is too steep, the wing will stall and drag goes way up and downforce drops dramatically. Check with the wing manufacturer about the ideal angle of attack and at what angle stall occurs.

Chapter Ten
Testing Handling

The slalom test is the most intense few seconds in all of automotive testing. *Jeff Cheechov*

The only way to really dial-in a suspension system and wheel and tire package is by testing. All tire companies test tires. Some suspension companies test suspension systems. The companies that do not test have packages that rarely perform as well as stock, often due to poor design, improper tuning, and excessive understeer or oversteer.

I've been testing tires, suspensions, and cars for 20 years for private companies as well as publications. Surprisingly—

or not—the same tuner car and suspension companies keep hitting home runs. But most tuner cars are mediocre at best and many suspension companies do not understand vehicle dynamics and tire traction. And the results show. The companies whose products are featured in this book all test, and they all understand dynamics and tire traction. They also understand the needs of consumers with varying performance priorities. There may be

other companies out there who undertake testing and create excellent packages, but I have not had the pleasure of driving and testing their products.

All of the testing I have been involved in has occurred at race tracks or testing facilities. While relatively safe in a controlled environment, testing would be very hazardous on public roads. If you have the opportunity to test on a track or test site, by all means do so, but never test on the street.

Slalom Course Testing

The most exciting 6-plus seconds in automotive testing is the slalom. The standard course is 600 feet long with traffic cones placed exactly 100 feet apart. Entry speed onto the course for most vehicles is 60 miles per hour. For a high-grip, nimble car, the entry speed can be as high as 70 miles per hour. The car (and driver) must make six directional changes through the six gates at the limits of traction, carrying the maximum speed possible without slowing too much, scrubbing off speed, or losing control. It is a true driving challenge and an extreme test of a vehicle's total traction and responsiveness.

Where the skid pad is a real test of tire traction, the straight-line slalom is the best indicator of overall handling balance and chassis responsiveness to driver inputs. If a car is fast and nimble in a slalom, it will work well under any circumstance.

Driving a slalom course requires intense concentration. There are three keys. First, timing steering inputs with releasing the throttle helps rotate the car into the new direction more quickly. But if your timing is off, you will lose speed. Second, minimal steering inputs are needed for reduced tire scrub and rapid vehicle response. Third, properly timed acceleration without too much throttle application allows maximum speed through the course. A fast slalom run requires six steering wheel inputs, six throttle lifts (possibly partial), and five smooth throttle applications, all perfectly timed.

The slalom can be a very dangerous exercise. If you have an opportunity to test on a slalom course, make sure there is a lot of acceleration room, at least 600 feet, lots of runoff area, at least 100 feet per side, and a minimum of 500 feet for braking. Make sure there is no cross-traffic. Always wear a helmet and driver restraints. Start out slowly and build up to speed gradually.

The skid pad is the best way to test tire grip and tune tire contact patches for optimum loading. Photo above: *Rick Herrick* Photo below: *Jeff Cheechov*

The Skid Pad

A skid pad is like a dyno for tires and suspensions. It's the most accurate way to measure cornering power, providing a true measure of cornering force over a measured distance and a sustained duration. A skid pad is a circular course laid out on asphalt or concrete. Lap times are taken for exactly one lap on the circle. For a known radius circle, a simple conversion formula allows lateral acceleration, or cornering force, to be determined in gs. One g is the force of gravity, or in scientific terms, an acceleration of 32.2 feet per second. Acceleration is defined as a change in velocity (speed) or a change in direction. We can measure straight-line acceleration (or deceleration), which is the rate in speed change. A 0-to-60-mile-per-hour acceleration or braking test is common for cars. And we can measure lateral acceleration, which is a change in direction and gives a very accurate measure of cornering power, much like a dyno gives an accurate measure of engine horsepower.

continued on page 100

Toyo Subjective Tire Test
Miyazaki Tire Proving Grounds, Japan

Wet braking was one of several tests conducted with the Toyota Arist V300 at Toyo Tires Miyazaki Proving Grounds in Japan.

I was asked to test tires at the Toyo Tires Miyazaki Proving Grounds in Japan, a rare opportunity to experience firsthand the procedures used by a major tire manufacturer to develop an ultra-high-performance tire. The purpose of the visit was to participate in a subjective comparison test of several ultra-high-performance (UHP) tires, including the new Toyo Proxes T1-S. The other three competitive tires were the Bridgestone Potenza S-02, the Dunlop SP9000, and the Goodyear Eagle F1. The tire size in all cases was 235/45R17, and the test vehicle in all tests was the Toyota Arist V300, which is sold in the United States as the Lexus GS300.

The test included wet traction and stability, dry handling and noise, and ride comfort. After an orientation and demonstration by the Toyo engineers and test drivers, I tested each of the tires on each of the courses.

The first exercise for each of the tires was the wet stability test. This included a pass at about 60 mph across a flooded skid pad area. If a tire were prone to aquaplaning, it would do so here.

None of the tires aquaplaned at the 60-mph speed. They all felt good in a straight-line. When steering inputs were added to the mix, some tires responded more quickly than others. The Toyo Proxes T1-S was

good, but the Bridgestone Potenza S-02 was the best. The Goodyear and Dunlop were also OK, but the Toyo was a little more responsive.

The 60-mph wet lane change yielded similar results. Impressions of the tires were mixed. None of the tires were like a wet compound race tire, but all of them were OK. The Toyo felt like it had really good grip, on par with the Bridgestone and better than the others. On the other hand, the Bridgestone felt more responsive to steering inputs. It felt like the Bridgestone was suited more to the Toyota Arist V300 than the Toyo, while the other tires were both less responsive and had lower levels of traction.

This was even more apparent on the wet traction segment. The wet traction course features a flooded corner that sweeps through an arc of more than 200 degrees and has a decreasing radius through the last third of the turn. Each test was conducted at 36-mph and each driver had three runs on each tire. The Bridgestone was tried first, and it made it through the course just fine at the designated speed. The Dunlop and Goodyear both lost traction immediately, unable to maintain grip even in the constant radius segment. At a reduced speed, those tires would break loose as the corner tightened up toward the end. The Bridgestone would slide slightly as the radius decreased, but it was very balanced. The Toyo T1-S was good all the way through, even entering the decreasing radius; but even though the slide was balanced when breakaway occurred, the Dunlop and Goodyear tires did not stay on course at 36 mph.

The Bridgestone and Toyo tires slid at 36 mph, but they did stay on course though the radius of the corner decreased. The Bridge-stones operated at a smaller slip angle than the Toyos but with slightly less feel. The Toyo took more steering lock to follow the same path. The Toyo provided good feedback, but it took some steering input. Both stayed on the road at 36-mph; it took more steering lock to hold the Toyota on the desired path in the corner.

The Toyo was good, but took more work to get through the turn at 36-mph. The Bridgestone was the best in the wet, but only slightly better than the Toyo T1-S. The Goodyear and the Dunlop entries were really good tires in the wet, but just did not have the level of grip or the feeling of control offered by the Toyo and the Bridgestone tires.

Where the wet-weather traction would be considered the most important test from a safety perspective, the dry handling and traction tests are the most significant from a performance standpoint. The dry handling track at the Miyazaki Proving Grounds is tight, with several long turns where maximum cornering g's are sustained for up to 270 degrees. The straight sections of the course offer speeds in the Toyota Arist V300 in excess of 75 miles per hour with a 70-plus-mph turn followed by threshold braking and tight turns.

The course can be run in either direction and offers a wide range of cornering situations, including some difficult transitions that really challenge a tire's responsiveness. Each tire was driven for three laps in each direction.

To be fair, all of the tires are excellent performers in the dry. On the road, the vast majority of drivers would be unable to determine a difference in traction levels. But we were lucky enough to get to try the tires on a test track, where there is no traffic and driving to the limits of adhesion is the point of the exercise. While the Dunlop and Goodyear were

excellent tires, they did not have the level of grip of the other tires. In each case they also were less responsive when transitioning from turns in one direction to the other. The Toyo tires were noticeably more responsive, while the Bridgestones felt a little better than the Toyos.

The Toyo also felt very precise on corner entry, especially under trail-braking situations. The Bridgestone tires had less understeer than the Toyo, even though maximum grip was a little less. This seemed to be the same feeling as in the wet, where the Bridgestone tires felt more suited to the Toyota Arist V300 platform than the Toyo T1-S. In the dry, however, the Toyo T1-S had more cornering speed. In part, this may have been made more apparent by the traction and stability control on the Toyota Arist.

The third segment of the subjective testing was on the noise and ride course. This part of the proving grounds provides several types of road surfaces and different types of bumps and ruts for both noise and ride tests.

Where the focus of a UHP tire test is performance, it would be a mistake

to ignore the ride and noise characteristics of these tires. The consumer must live with these characteristics for the life of a tire, and an overly harsh ride or loud, annoying noise levels can detract from the enjoyment of the purchase.

Over my 20 years of testing tires and suspension components for street and racing applications, I never had tested noise and ride. This was a new experience for me and one I welcomed.

Each tire was driven over a course on the test track designed to provide varying surface materials and degrees of roughness. All of the tires are somewhat harsh by nature. Low-profile UHP tires are supposed to be rigid, and rigid is less conducive to ride comfort. I am clearly not qualified to be a critic in the ride and noise tests, but the Goodyear Eagle F1 and the Toyo Proxes T1-S were more comfortable over the bumps and ruts. It's hard to quantify this, but they just felt better than the Bridgestone and the Dunlop. If ride is somewhat esoteric for the performance-oriented test driver, noise is even more so.

Before this test, I would have only noticed noise on the highway

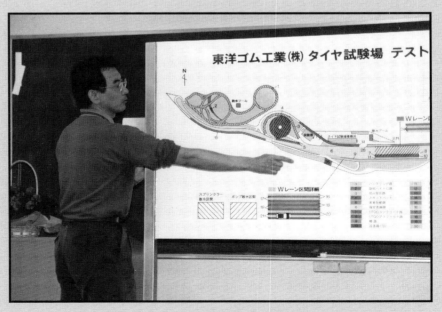

A Toyo test engineer points out features of the Miyazaki test facility prior to on-track tests.

and only if it was really annoying. In fact, that is still my level of sophistication: a tire's noise quality is either acceptable or annoying. This is clearly an area where my ears need a more thorough education. But I could at least tell a difference.

The Toyo Proxes T1-S and the Bridgestone Potenza S-02 were nearly equal—not annoying, but not the quieteist tires in the test. The Goodyear had the most acceptable noise level, or maybe it was sound quality and noise level combined. The Dunlop SP Sport 9000 was actually annoying; it was too loud and the frequency was unpleasant to me. The Toyo test drivers and engineers have many years of experience, as well as instrumentation to evaluate noise levels and frequencies. Overall, the Goodyear gets the nod in the ride and noise department, with the Toyo second. The Bridgestone and Dunlop were about equal.

In the final analysis, there was not a slouch in this group. Every tire is high quality, and for the average UHP tire consumer, little difference would be noticed from one tire to another. If the buyer were leaning toward the most comfortable tire, the Goodyear would be my choice, but only by a small margin. If wet-weather traction were the most important criterion, then the Bridgestone would have a small advantage. If dry traction were the key element, the Toyo Proxes T1-S would be my pick. Personally, my priorities for a UHP tire are dry traction, then wet traction, with ride a minor consideration and noise almost not a factor.

The Proving Grounds

Tire testing and development requires sound engineering and scientific methods for worthwhile results. Among the Japanese tire manufacturers, Toyo Tire was first to recognize the importance of testing. In the early 1970s, Toyo constructed the first dedicated tire proving

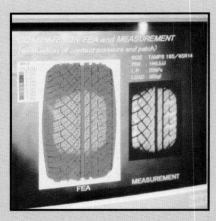

Toyo conducts computer-aided design and static machine testing of tires at its Itami Technical Center near Osaka, Japan.

grounds in Japan. Located in southern Japan near the east coast resort area of Miyazaki, the Toyo Tire Proving Grounds is a key link in the development of the highest-quality, best-performing tire possible.

Considering that Toyo uses cutting-edge computer technology in tire development, one might think that a tire proving ground was no longer necessary. In fact, because of the advanced computer technology, proving grounds are even more important. Data from the Miyazaki Proving Grounds was instrumental in the creation of the modeling for Toyo's Dynamic Simulation Optimized Contact II (DSOC II) software. Continued track testing and data gathering allows Toyo engineers to confirm the validity of the computer models and add a continual data stream to the research. This allows even more accurate modeling for future designs.

Miyazaki allows tire test engineers to evaluate the performance of a tire in several critical areas. Dry traction, wet traction, braking performance, responsiveness, durability, wear, ride, and noise are all factors affecting the quality and performance of a tire. Toyo engineers can gather real-world, real-time data in each critical category.

The Miyazaki facility allows engineers to test any tire under any condition. Wet and dry skid pads, handling courses, special low-friction corners, and large asphalt "black lake" areas put test drivers and engineers in real but controlled-friction situations. This gives feedback and consistency important for accurate evaluation of traction and handling characteristics. No amount of electronic test equipment or computer modeling can confirm important criteria the way a rigorous test program can, and Toyo has been at it longer than any Japanese tire manufacturer.

Specific tests are designed to evaluate tire performance, quality, ride, and comfort. At Miyazaki, Toyo engineers evaluate wet traction using special areas where controlled flooding allows standardized testing. Hydroplaning, wet braking grip, wet cornering grip, responsiveness, and stability are evaluated. Dry traction is evaluated on a handling course, dry skid pad, lane change, braking area, and slalom. Responsiveness and stability are both monitored during wet and dry traction testing. Noise and ride are evaluated on specialized areas of the proving grounds where real road conditions are simulated. Wear and durability are constantly monitored throughout all phases of testing.

An additional winter proving grounds located at Hokkaido in northern Japan allows Toyo engineers to evaluate snow and ice traction and performance. Additional testing is undertaken in Germany and the United States. Toyo's involvement in motorsports around the globe brings an additional element and important data to the intensive Toyo engineering effort.

Continuing focus on research, development, engineering, and testing allows the premier tire manufacturers to bring the best product possible to the marketplace.

Toyo Tire Itami Technical Center Overview

On the leading edge of tire technology, Toyo Tires has developed advanced computer modeling and testing at its Itami Technical Center near Osaka, Japan. At Itami, tire engineers have taken every design element of a tire, from compounding to tread design to sidewall construction, to create computer modeling software for further development. Toyo's system is called Dynamic Simulation Optimized Contact II (DSOC II). Run on a CRAY Supercomputer, this second-generation Toyo modeling computer software allows complete multiaxis movement as well as sidewall and contact patch deformation within the computer. This advanced and unique technology allows engineers to create new products in a very short time frame.

By combining every element of tire design, including silica-based compounding and sidewall construction, the DSOC II technology allows outstanding wear, wet weather, and dry traction characteristics to be combined in a single product, such as the new Toyo Proxes T1-S Ultra-High-Performance Tire.

After the computer-aided design and prototyping, the tires are subjected to a series of intense laboratory tests at the Itami Technical Center. Tests conducted in the lab include the High-Speed Drum Tester, which can simulate road speeds of more than 250 miles per hour.

By monitoring temperatures, engineers can determine heat buildup characteristics up to the speed of tire failure. This ensures that a tire design easily exceeds its speed rating. The tire contact patch can be observed under rotational and lateral loading. The contact patch pressure distribution can by measured and photographed. By monitoring contact patch pressure under a variety of vertical and lateral loads, tire sidewall design data is correlated to contact patch pressure data. Data is used in the DSOC II files and integrated into the computer-aided design process. This ensures optimum contact patch performance that is crucial to all tire designs, but it's especially important for the ultra-high-performance tire category.

The Toyo Proxes T1-S was yet to be released in the U.S. when testing was conducted in Japan.

One of the most intriguing tests at the center is the Flat-Trac II Cornering Test Machine. As the name implies, this machine allows cornering tests on the flat surface of a moving simulated road. The machine can test variable loads as well as steering angle inputs. This testing allows Toyo engineers to accurately determine slip angle characteristics, traction, and contact patch deformation under real-world cornering situations. Toyo also uses a more traditional Tire Cornering Test Machine that uses a rotating drum for testing. This provides another source of critical data for the DSOC II simulation, as well as data to confirm the performance of a prototype design.

Tire vibration is analyzed in the lab with a Fourier Systems Computer-Aided Tire Vibration Mode Analysis test. This test determines vibration characteristics relating to both rotational speed and potential vibration inputs from road surfaces. Again, this data allows testing of a prototype design as well as data collection for the DSOC II simulation program.

Noise is an important characteristic in tire design. Noise tests at the Itami Technical Center include exterior noise levels and frequencies as well as interior noise levels over a variety of road speeds and surface conditions. Other tests conducted in the engineering lab include Rolling Resistance and Bead Unseating Force. These tests are important for fuel economy and safety.

Research and development are critical steps in the tire manufacturing process. At Itami, Toyo scientists are constantly working on new polymers and materials to improve traction and tire life as well as environmental qualities of tire compounds. In addition to the Toyo engineers' ability to formulate compounds, a series of high-tech equipment is used for analysis and testing. Included in the lab are sophisticated pieces of equipment such as an electron microscope, a Fourier Infrared Absorption Photometer, a Lambourn Abrasion Tester, a Visco Elastic Spectrometer, Strip Bi-axial Tester, and a Belt Fatigue Tester. Each of these devices helps Toyo scientists and engineers determine the viability of new materials and polymers for specific tire applications. Collected data is used to analyze effectiveness and improve modeling for the DSOC II simulation software.

After a prototype is developed and tested at the Itami Technical Center, a full test program is undertaken at the Miyazaki Proving Grounds and, for four-season designs, the Hokkaido Winter Testing facility in northern Japan. Intensive tests are carried out at these facilities to confirm the design parameters before a new tire is put into production. Once in production, tires are selected at random for further laboratory and track testing.

Brake testing is valuable for overall performance, but with antilock brake systems, this is the easiest test for the driver. *Jeff Donker*

Continued from page 95

> The formula for converting a lap time to a g force is
>
> G force = $\dfrac{\text{radius of circle (feet)} \times 1.225}{\text{time (seconds)}}$.

The standard radius for testing is 100 feet, though any radius from about 80 feet to 300 feet will work.

Driving on a skid pad is more difficult than it looks. It's like walking a tightrope. Too much steering and you scrub off critical speed. Too much throttle and you can spin the tires or even pick up a strong push, depending on the car. The trick is to make steering and throttle adjustments as small as possible. An interesting point is a more powerful car is easier to drive because the power can be used to overcome handling problems. An underpowered car, such as the Civic project car, requires a perfect setup to be fast.

Skid Pad and Data Acquisition

Modern computer technology and data acquisition systems provide an excellent means of recording data. The problem with data acquisition for measuring maximum traction is that data points are taken every 100th of a second (or more). This gives us a traction reading for only a very short time span and over a tiny distance. The distance a single data point is measured across is about 1/2 foot. The traction over that 1/2 foot can be as much as 7 percent higher or lower than the average over one 655-foot lap. A single data point or "spike" can be misleading. Sustaining cornering power over one period of 10 plus seconds and 655 feet provides a true picture of real traction. For this reason, skid pad testing offers the only really accurate measure of cornering force. And the best, most accurate test is the two-way average, taking times on both clockwise and counterclockwise laps.

Braking Test

The easiest of the standard tests is braking. Most modern cars feature antilock brake systems, so driver skill is not tested much. Cars without ABS offer a greater challenge. Brake testing allows fine-tuning of the brake system, or the opportunity to try new rotors, calipers, or brake pad compounds. Most tests are from 60 miles per hour to 0, with the stopping distance measured in feet. A fifth-wheel data logger or radar are the most accurate ways to measure stopping distance.

Important information includes not only stopping distance, but wheel lock-up at one wheel or one axle and brake fade over a series of several stops. Wheel lock up can ruin braking performance, especially if only one wheel or one pair of wheels at one end locks up early. One-wheel lock-up is usually caused by a mechanical problem at the caliper. Lock-up at one end is usually caused by brake bias problems. Brake fade can be caused by improper brake pad compounds or boiling brake fluid. See the brake chapter for more details. Testing and problem solving can pay big performance dividends and improve safety.

The Test Track

If you drive on a race track, rally course, or autocross, an ideal place to do skid pad, slalom, and brake testing is on the course itself. Even a street vehicle can benefit from a track-day test session. For that reason, the suspension companies that test also test on the track, even for street packages. It's safer, and the controlled environment allows the best possible tuning of the package for a wide variety of conditions.

If you compete, testing is important. If you want the optimum street performance, select packages from companies that test them for you. For more information on tuning suspension while testing, see the appropriate chapters.

The final answers come from track testing, especially for motorsports applications. *Bob Schroeder*

Chapter Eleven
Tuning with Tires

There are several ways to alter handling balance. You can change spring rates, bar rates, cross-weight, suspension geometry, shock rates, roll center location, tire pressure, or static weight distribution. But handling balance is only part of the story. The goal for any racing situation is to get maximum traction from the tires—we hope that's all of the tires. Each tire is capable of making so much traction on a given car and under given track conditions. Nothing you do can cause the tires to make more traction than that limit. But how you tune the chassis and work the tire contact patches will determine how much traction you actually have available. The goal is to minimize the loss. A key way to do this is to optimize the tire's contact with the track surface and optimize the load on all four contact patches relative to a given spot on the race track, mid-turn, corner entry, or corner exit. While not a factor for street driving, any form of motorsports competition requires the optimization of tire traction at each tire contact patch and at the highest possible level of grip from all four tires.

So how do you know what's going on? The best measure of tire traction is temperature. Tire pyrometers are inexpensive, easy to use, and the single most important tool you can own to get a car setup dialed-in. But there are some techniques you need to know to get the best possible data.

Measuring Tire Temperatures

The following are some important tips for tire temperature measurements:

• Always record temperatures, even if the car is out only for one or two laps.

The only way to understand how a tire is loaded dynamically is to know the temperatures of the tires across the surface of the tread.

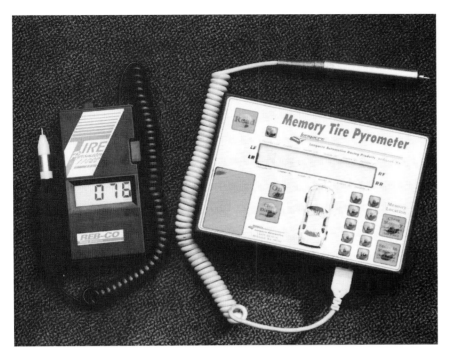

Many types of pyrometers are available. The memory pyrometer on the right stores data for later retrieval and analysis. The best pyrometers get up to temperature the most quickly. The pyrometer is the most important piece of setup equipment you can use.

- Take temps after the event when possible.
- Record pressures as well as temperatures.
- Use a tire temperature chart.
- Take temps at three spots on each tire about 1 inch from each edge and in the middle.
- Always take temps in the same lateral spot on the tire tread.
- Always take temps in the same order on the tire (either inside or outside first, then the middle).
- Always start at the same tire.
- Always go around the car in the same direction.
- Move fast. Tires cool quickly, giving inaccurate readings if too much time elapses. The heat will also equalize across the tire. The temperature difference grows smaller as time passes.
- While moving fast is important, make sure that each reading has stabilized before moving the probe to the next spot. Removing

the probe from a spot too soon can cause inaccurate readings.
- Unless you use a memory pyrometer, have one crew member record temps while the other takes the readings. If no crew member is available, the driver can record the data while sitting in the car.
- The fourth tire in the sequence will lose heat by the time its temps are taken. After measuring the fourth tire, check the first tire again so that you can see the drop in temps from the first readings. This will give you an idea of how hot the other tires were while the first tire was being checked. This is an important part of the procedure.
- Take tire pressures right after taking the temperatures. Go in the same order. Also record pressures just before the car goes onto the race track so that you can measure the pressure gain.
- Once in a while, check tire pressures after 5 to 10 minutes. If the

pressure is higher than when the car entered the pits, the extra heat causing the pressure has come from the brakes. Tires have been known to blow out (a long time ago) while sitting in the pits due to temperature and pressure buildup from brake heat. If the pressures go up, you have a potential brake heat problem.
- The needle on the probe should be inserted into the tire tread. The heat is more stable and cools more slowly below the tread surface.
- Keep heat in the probe by holding your thumb or finger over the needle while taking the temps.
- Slide the probe over the tire tread surface when moving the probe across the tire. This keeps the probe hot and reduces the time necessary to get the peak temperature.
- A higher-priced pyrometer often has a more sensitive probe, reducing time to get up to temperature.
- Using more than one pyrometer can get temps faster and give more accurate readings.
- Taking tire temperatures at different locations around the track will give you different information about what the tires are doing under different conditions of braking, cornering, or accelerating. This can prove to be very helpful in solving handling problems at different points on the track.
- The driver should avoid hard braking coming into the pits (or wherever the tire temps are taken). The hard braking will put excessive heat in the front tires compared to the rear.
- The driver should not take a cool-down lap. The tires will cool too quickly, giving false readings.

Taking tire temperatures is a crucial link in the chassis-tuning process. Be religious about taking temps and recording the appropriate information. It will come in handy.

Using an Infrared Pyrometer

One of the latest innovations in setup equipment is the infrared pyrometer. Its biggest advantage is speed. The biggest drawback is consistency. Infrared averages heat over the area within the field of view of its lens. The area the lens reads is proportional to the distance the lens is held from the heat source. Since we need to monitor as little as 1 degree of temperature differential from one spot to the next on a tire, if too large an area is read, or if the area is inconsistent in size, then the data is less useful. It is important to hold an infrared pyrometer at the exact same distance from the tread surface every time you use it. And it needs to be held close enough to the tread so that a spot only about 1 inch wide is monitored.

Keep in mind that an infrared pyrometer reads temps very quickly, but it reads the surface temp only, and the surface cools and its temperature balances more quickly than the rubber below the surface

Chassis-Tuning Techniques Using Tire Temperatures

Your racecar is perfectly balanced through the corners. It gets into the turns quickly, and corner exit is strong, but you consistently lose two car lengths in mid-turn. Toe is correct, roll couple seems good, cross-weights seem right. What could cause the car to be slow in midturn? The answer is a lack of total traction.

The goal when you set up your racecar is to get maximum traction as well as create a good balance all the way around the race track. If, for some reason, maximum traction is not there, the car will not perform to its peak at

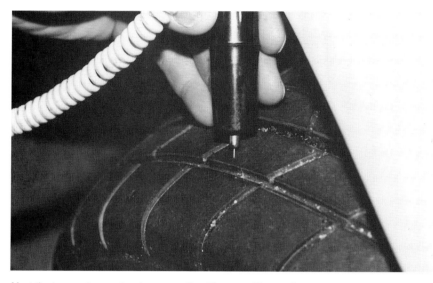

Most tire temperature probes have a needle with a stop. The needle should be inserted into the tire tread up to the stop.

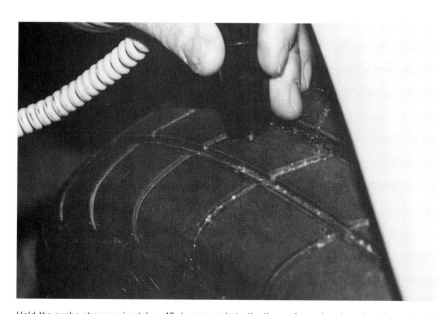

Hold the probe at approximately a 45-degree angle to the tire surface when inserting the probe into the tread. Hold your finger over the probe needle to keep heat in the needle as you move the probe across the tire tread.

FRONT

10 11 12   3 2 1

ORDER FOR TAKING TIRE TEMPERATURES

7 8 9   6 5 4

Always start at the same tire and move around the car in the same direction every time. It is useful to take the first tire's temperatures a second time so you can see the temperature drop between the first reading and the reading after the fourth tire temps are taken. This will give you a better idea of the temp drop from the first to second tire readings, second to third, and third to fourth tire readings. This allows interpolation of temperatures if the change is significant.

some point on, or all the way around, the race track. A few tricks for obtaining maximum traction follow:

1. Consider All Four Tires.

The goal is to get the most traction possible from all four tires. The harder each tire works, the more traction the car will have, and the faster the car can enter, get through, and exit the corners. One sign of how hard a tire is working (and therefore the tire's traction) is the average temperature of the tire. There are two types of tire temperature averages: the average for a single tire and the average of pairs of tires like diagonal, side, or end. If the average temperature for a single tire is higher than the maximum temperature for your other tires, that tire is working too hard. If the average temperature is lower than that of the other tires, then that tire is not doing enough work.

Comparing average tire temperatures can offer a wealth of information.
• The cold tire needs to work harder.
• The hotter end of the car is losing traction before the colder end. If the rear average temp is hotter than the front, the car is oversteering; if the front average is hotter, the car is understeering. This could indicate a change in roll couple distribution (spring rates or sway bar rates).
• If one side (left or right) has an average tire temperature hotter than the other side, more static weight on the cooler side would help.
• Diagonal average tire temps will offer clues about cross-weights for a given situation.

2. Look at the Complete Tire Contact Patch.

The individual temperatures at different points on a given tire offer solid information about what is happening at the tire contact patch.
• If an edge of a tire is hotter, the camber is off.
• If the middle of the tire is hotter or colder, the pressure is off.

3. Always Take Tire Temperatures.

Tire temps are the only link you have to what is happening at the tire contact patch. You need to know what is happening, so always take tire temps, even after a race.

4. Measure Tire Temperatures at Different Locations on the Race Track.

The habit is to take tire temps in the pits. On a test day, you may be able to take tire temps at any point on the race track. This can give you important information about what the tires are doing under a variety of conditions. For example, if you measure temps coming off a corner, you will see how

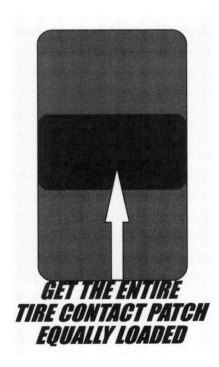

GET THE ENTIRE TIRE CONTACT PATCH EQUALLY LOADED

The first goal is get the entire contact patch of each tire equally loaded across the tread surface.

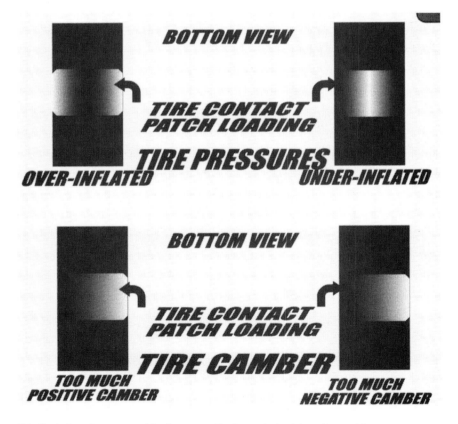

BOTTOM VIEW

TIRE CONTACT PATCH LOADING

TIRE PRESSURES

OVER-INFLATED   UNDER-INFLATED

BOTTOM VIEW

TIRE CONTACT PATCH LOADING

TIRE CAMBER

TOO MUCH POSITIVE CAMBER   TOO MUCH NEGATIVE CAMBER

This illustration shows unequal loading across the tire contact patch surface and the cause.

ATTEMPT TO
GET THE LOADS
ON ALL FOUR
CONTACT PATCHES
EQUAL

The final goal is to get the contact patches at each corner as close to equally loaded as possible.

the tires are working at this critical point on the track. Naturally, the rear tires should be hotter in this situation, just as the fronts should be hotter under hard braking. Keep the following facts in mind when taking tire temps at various points:

- When you stop to take temps, slow gently or too much heat will build in the front tires, unless you are measuring corner entry temps.
- When you analyze temps, take into account where you took the temps.
- Midturn setup is best when all tire temps are close to equal.
- Front temps should be hotter at corner entry, but as close to equal left-to-right as possible.
- Drive wheel tires should be equal but hotter than fronts at corner exit.

5. Consider Static Weight Distribution.

One way to get average tire temps closer together and to increase total traction is to look at the temps and compare them to static weight distribution. If a tire is more than 15 to 20 degrees cooler, that tire needs more static weight on it. More static weight

on a cold tire means more dynamic weight on the same tire while cornering and less on another tire. This will most often improve overall traction, although handling balance may need to be re-established.

6. Consider Dynamic Weight Distribution.

The goal is to have dynamic weight distribution as equal as possible at rest so that the average tire load is the same during left and right turns. Tire temps can give you the same basic information and allow you to make good judgments about improving setup.

7. Consider Tire Heat.

If the tire has heat, it's making traction, up to the point where the tire gets too hot. When all the tires are in the optimum operating temperature range, you are getting maximum traction. Anything less than that indicates your racecar could be getting around the track faster. The following are some important facts to keep in mind:

- If any tire is overheated, it is doing too much work. A change is needed.
- If all tires are overheated, the compound may be too soft for the car and conditions.
- If the front tires are overheating, the driver may be using the brakes too hard while steering.
- If the driven tires are overheating, the driver may be using too much throttle exiting the corners, causing wheelspin.
- If temps are too cool overall, it could be the ambient weather conditions. If it's cold, take that into account.
- If average temps are too cold, it could be the driver. If the driver is not up to speed, temps will never get to optimum and handling problems should be nearly nonexistent. The driver needs to push the car closer to the limits of traction before any setup issue can be resolved with any clarity.

8. Heat the Tires Properly.

If a tire is colder than the rest, figure out how to get more heat there. Following are some tips:

- Start with static weight distribution. Put weight on the cold tire without sacrificing the overall vertical load balance of the car as a whole.
- If the front or rear is colder, put more roll couple distribution (stiffer springs/bars) at the colder end.
- If the diagonal average temperatures are off, check cross-weights.
- Toe and bump steer can generate heat on the inside of the front tires. What happens at the tire contact patch is all we really care about when trying to get the maximum traction from a racecar. Nothing else really matters. Tire temperatures are the easiest and most cost-effective link you have to the action at the tire contact patch. Using the tire temperatures effectively can pay considerable dividends on the race track. It's worth the effort.

Chassis Tuning with Average Tire Temperatures

At your home track, you're fast, but you cannot maintain quite as much cornering speed as your closest competitor. He goes through midturn and the turn exits just a little bit faster. You've been monitoring tire temperatures all season, and the temps look good. All of the inside temps are just a little hotter than the outside, and the middle temps are right in between. Pressures and camber are dialed. What else can you do?

You know that tire temperatures offer clues about traction at each tire contact patch, but what about comparing one tire, or pair of tires, to the others? The average tire temps are another clue you can use to find more traction.

Average tire temperatures are found for each tire by adding the three temp readings together then dividing by 3. In addition to the average temperature at each tire, you will want to know the average temperatures for the left side and right side, the front and the rear, and the two diagonals. The goal is to get the average temps at each tire as close to each other as possible. This means that each tire is doing as much work as possible. If one tire is much hotter, or cooler, then tuning may make your car faster.

What average tire temperature clues can tell you is the effectiveness of static weight distribution, how cross-weight is affecting the car, if the roll couple distribution is in the ballpark, brake balance, how the driver is using the controls, and if there may be chassis alignment problems.

Always look at the individual temps because they will still tell you how well that tire contact patch is working on the track surface. Use the individual temps to tune pressures first, then adjust.

The following are some examples of tire temps and their interpretation:

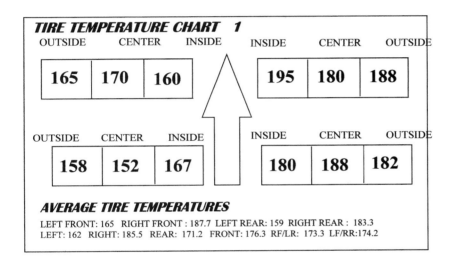

Tire Temperature Chart 1

This chart shows pressures that are not correct. The right front pressure is too low, the left front is too high, the left rear is too low, and the right rear is too high. It takes practice to determine how much to change the pressure for a given set of conditions. The greater the difference, the greater the change needs to be to get the contact patch flat on the race track. Keep in mind that when the center temp is hotter, the pressure is too high, and if the center temp is cooler, the pressure is too low.

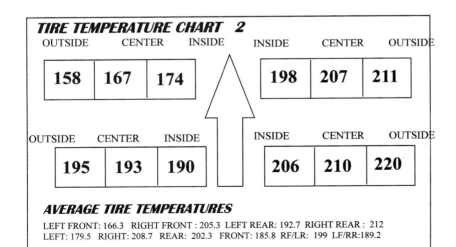

Tire Temperature Chart 2

The front camber is off in this chart. At the left front, the wheel needs less negative camber to heat the outside edge of the tire. The right front needs more negative camber. Since tires make the most traction in a corner with a small amount of dynamic negative camber, the inside edges of the front tires should show temps between 5 and 10 degrees hotter than the outside edges. This indicates that the tire is getting maximum traction.

Tire Temperature Chart 3

The left rear is in the ballpark, with the inside a little hotter than the outside. The right rear is the opposite, which is undesirable. The rear axle, if solid, could be bent or out of alignment. With independent rear suspension, the right needs more negative camber. Both fronts could use more negative camber, and the left front could use a little more load. But be careful. These temps were taken in the pit area after a run and the last turn was a left-hander; the left-side temps are both a little lower than the right side and the left turn is the likely reason.

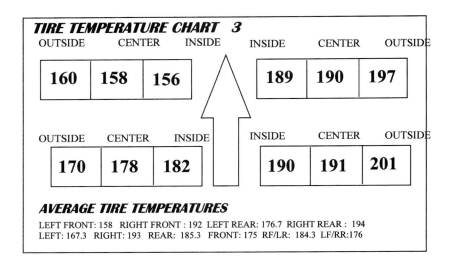

Tire Temperature Chart 4

Look at the front tire temps, which are nearly perfect at first glance. This temperature pattern can be caused by too much toe-out at the front. The camber, which looks good here, could be off, costing tire traction, but the excessive toe out masks the real problem. For this reason, it is important to routinely check toe. A slight bump or wear can change toe settings and hide other problems.

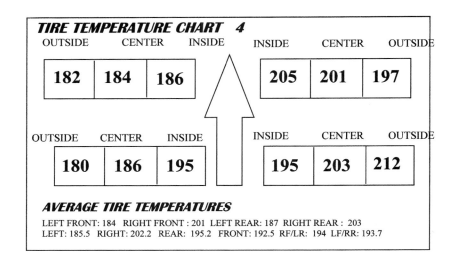

Tire Temperature Chart 5

Roll steer, or rear axle steer, can cause temperature patterns like those shown here. This causes scrub and heats the leading edge of the tire contact patch. Even though the average temperatures show that the car should be oversteering, this car probably understeers in left turns and oversteers in right turns. Checking rear axle alignment and cross-weights will tell you how to cure the situation. The most important thing is to not be fooled by the data. You need to know what the rear suspension is doing so you can make better judgments about the setup.

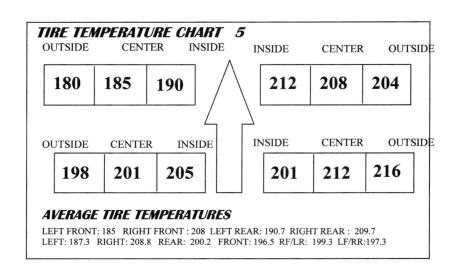

108

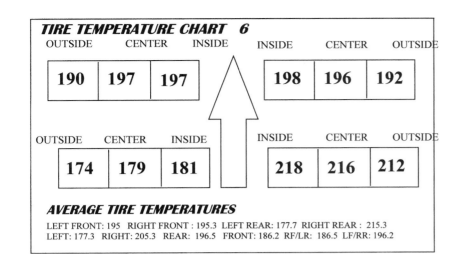

TIRE TEMPERATURE CHART 6

OUTSIDE	CENTER	INSIDE		INSIDE	CENTER	OUTSIDE
190	197	197		198	196	192

OUTSIDE	CENTER	INSIDE		INSIDE	CENTER	OUTSIDE
174	179	181		218	216	212

AVERAGE TIRE TEMPERATURES

LEFT FRONT: 195 RIGHT FRONT : 195.3 LEFT REAR: 177.7 RIGHT REAR : 215.3
LEFT: 177.3 RIGHT: 205.3 REAR: 196.5 FRONT: 186.2 RF/LR: 186.5 LF/RR: 196.2

Tire Temperature Chart 6

Here is a rear-drive car that is well set up except for one thing. The last corner was a left-hand turn. Wheelspin caused the higher right rear temps. The driver needs to be smoother on the accelerator, but the car also could use a limited-slip differential. Keep in mind that many factors must be considered. The average temps are indicators, not the final word.

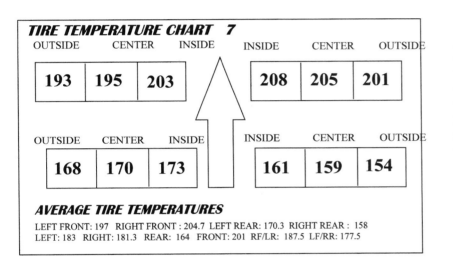

TIRE TEMPERATURE CHART 7

OUTSIDE	CENTER	INSIDE		INSIDE	CENTER	OUTSIDE
193	195	203		208	205	201

OUTSIDE	CENTER	INSIDE		INSIDE	CENTER	OUTSIDE
168	170	173		161	159	154

AVERAGE TIRE TEMPERATURES

LEFT FRONT: 197 RIGHT FRONT : 204.7 LEFT REAR: 170.3 RIGHT REAR : 158
LEFT: 183 RIGHT: 181.3 REAR: 164 FRONT: 201 RF/LR: 187.5 LF/RR: 177.5

Tire Temperature Chart 7

Here is a front-drive car with an excellent setup. The only improvement would be more heat in the rear tires, but with the front weight bias, that would be very difficult to do, and would actually hurt lap times, since load would be removed from the front tires and corner exit traction would be reduced.

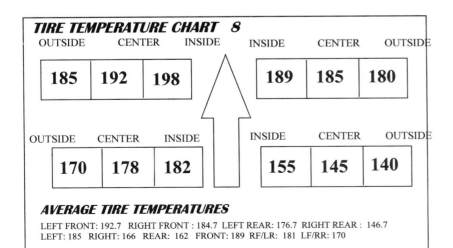

TIRE TEMPERATURE CHART 8

OUTSIDE	CENTER	INSIDE		INSIDE	CENTER	OUTSIDE
185	192	198		189	185	180

OUTSIDE	CENTER	INSIDE		INSIDE	CENTER	OUTSIDE
170	178	182		155	145	140

AVERAGE TIRE TEMPERATURES

LEFT FRONT: 192.7 RIGHT FRONT : 184.7 LEFT REAR: 176.7 RIGHT REAR : 146.7
LEFT: 185 RIGHT: 166 REAR: 162 FRONT: 189 RF/LR: 181 LF/RR: 170

Tire Temperature Chart 8

This is a front-drive car with a good setup, but the much colder right rear average temp shows that the right rear is nearly unloaded in a left turn. The pit area is just after a long left sweeper. It's very common for a front-driver to have enough roll resistance in the rear to lift the inside rear tire off the track surface in a corner. Beware of this when analyzing tire temps.

Tire Temperature Chart 9

The 31-degree-hotter front average on this rear-drive car shows understeer and indicates that the front roll couple percentage is too high. In other words, the front has too much roll resistance. The front springs could be softened, but a softer front antiroll bar would be a better choice, since it will not change the control of the tire contact patch over bumps. But the best choice in this instance would be a stiffer rear setup, with a stiffer antiroll bar or springs. The reason to change the rear instead of the front is that the front average tire temps are at the optimum temperature while the rear averages are cooler than optimum. The stiffer rear setup will put more load on the rear tires. In this example, the last turn on the track was a left turn, causing the right-side tires to be hotter.

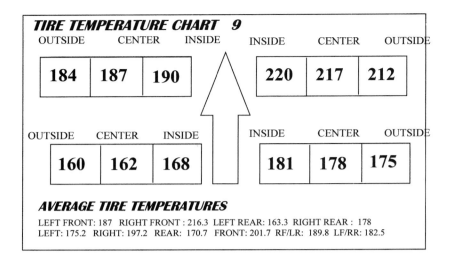

TIRE TEMPERATURE CHART 9

OUTSIDE	CENTER	INSIDE		INSIDE	CENTER	OUTSIDE
184	187	190		220	217	212

OUTSIDE	CENTER	INSIDE		INSIDE	CENTER	OUTSIDE
160	162	168		181	178	175

AVERAGE TIRE TEMPERATURES

LEFT FRONT: 187 RIGHT FRONT : 216.3 LEFT REAR: 163.3 RIGHT REAR : 178
LEFT: 175.2 RIGHT: 197.2 REAR: 170.7 FRONT: 201.7 RF/LR: 189.8 LF/RR: 182.5

Tire Temperature Chart 10

This is the opposite situation from Chart 9. In this case, the front bar could be stiffened a little, or the rear spring rates lowered a little, since all of the tires are within a good operating range.

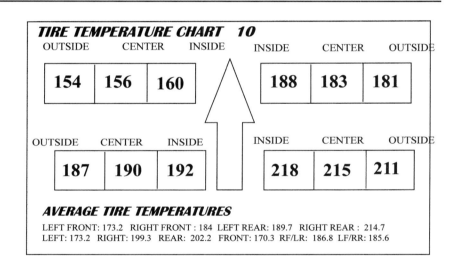

TIRE TEMPERATURE CHART 10

OUTSIDE	CENTER	INSIDE		INSIDE	CENTER	OUTSIDE
154	156	160		188	183	181

OUTSIDE	CENTER	INSIDE		INSIDE	CENTER	OUTSIDE
187	190	192		218	215	211

AVERAGE TIRE TEMPERATURES

LEFT FRONT: 173.2 RIGHT FRONT : 184 LEFT REAR: 189.7 RIGHT REAR : 214.7
LEFT: 173.2 RIGHT: 199.3 REAR: 202.2 FRONT: 170.3 RF/LR: 186.8 LF/RR: 185.6

Tire Temperature Chart 11

This is case of extreme understeer or push. In this case the driver has applied too much brake for the amount of steering lock being used, and the situation only gets worse in midturn and at exit as the throttle is applied, still with too much steering lock for the amount the other controls are being used.

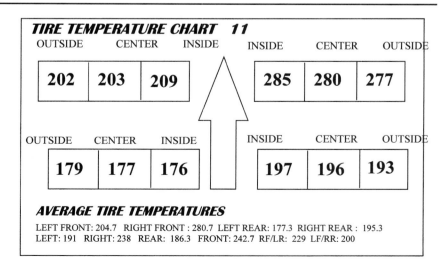

TIRE TEMPERATURE CHART 11

OUTSIDE	CENTER	INSIDE		INSIDE	CENTER	OUTSIDE
202	203	209		285	280	277

OUTSIDE	CENTER	INSIDE		INSIDE	CENTER	OUTSIDE
179	177	176		197	196	193

AVERAGE TIRE TEMPERATURES

LEFT FRONT: 204.7 RIGHT FRONT : 280.7 LEFT REAR: 177.3 RIGHT REAR : 195.3
LEFT: 191 RIGHT: 238 REAR: 186.3 FRONT: 242.7 RF/LR: 229 LF/RR: 200

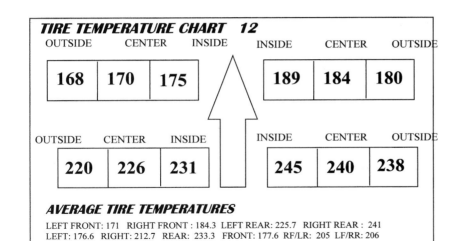

Tire Temperature Chart 12

This case looks like an extreme loose condition, but the car was neutral. The real problem was way too much rear-brake bias. The brake master cylinders had been reversed, making adjustments ineffective.

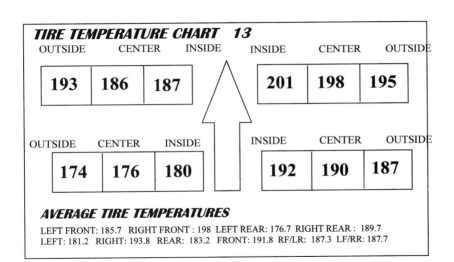

Tire Temperature Chart 13

On a rear-driver, when you see temps like these, and you know that all the settings are dialed, sit back and smile. You have achieved a really sound setup. Now work to keep it that way.

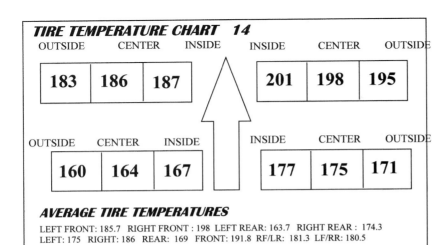

Tire Temperature Chart 14

On a front-driver, this is about as good as it gets. Work to keep the temps this good.

Chapter Twelve
Tuning Handling

The first job when tuning handling is to determine the source of the problem. Testing is the best way to get to that point. *Jeff Donker*

At the race, you're unloaded and ready to go for the first practice session. After the session is over, you feel lost because the handling is way off. You make changes that should help, but in the next session, the car feels even worse. The same scenario continues for the remainder of the event, and you're very unhappy with the result. Any one of the following problems could be your undoing.

One key to being fast and competitive is repeatability. You just cannot repeat results if you do not know where to start. A good chassis baseline is the one recommended by a prep shop. If you have the experience, create your own baseline. And best of all, if you have records from earlier races at the track you are going to, it gives you a head start. You should have the

following: frame heights, cross-weight percentage, rear and left-side weight percentages, all four tire circumferences, fuel load, gear ratio, spring rates, bar neutralized, shock valving, toe, rear alignment, pinion angle, panhard bar height or Watt's linkage settings, and any other setting affecting the handling.

Preparing the Car at the Track

This happens too often. You run out of time or have inadequate help before a test or race, so you end up preparing the car at the track, or at least finishing the job there. It is difficult to create a good setup at the track. It is easier and much more effective in the garage. Track time is expensive for a test day. Wasting that time is not effective. If you're prepping your car at a race, forget any chance of a good result.

Taking Tire Temperatures

Tire temperatures are your link to what goes on between the tire contact patch and the track surface. I find it difficult to make sound tuning decisions without tire temps. Tire temperatures should be taken every time the car comes in after a run on the track, even after a race.

Taking Segment Times

Time around the track is gained in very small increments. Chassis adjustments can make a car faster (or slower) around the track, but may cost time in certain areas of the race track. Knowing this can add to the data available for you to make sound tuning choices. The only way to accomplish this is to record times in several segments of the race track. You don't need to take times in every segment on every lap, but taking segments at various points for each session will prove valuable, especially in testing.

Crossweight Is Off

Crossweight, the measure of right front and left rear combined weight versus total car weight (both with driver), is a useful tuning tool. In road racing or autocrossing situations, excessive crossweight will help handling in one direction but hurt in the other, and it hurts more one way than it helps the other way. Crossweight should be set at 50 percent and never less than 49.5 percent or more than 50.5 percent.

Keeping Records

This may be the most costly sin of all. There is just too much data to keep track of without writing everything down in an organized way. Even if you get a good setup, without records you will be unable to repeat the setup without going through the complete process all over again. The most important time to keep track of records is back in the shop after a race. If you have a good race setup, this will tell you how to get back to the setup the next time you race at that track under similar circumstances. And if the results were not so good, at least you know you need to do something different.

Too Much Information

To achieve success it is imperative that you learn enough to make your own tuning decisions within your own team. Listening to advice from others is one thing, putting it to use is another. Even if the person offering advice is very knowledgeable, that person likely does not know your situation, preferences, resources, or needs. It's difficult to give advice that is useful to someone else. And most often, the person offering advice is less knowledgeable than you are, and usually only knows a couple of things that could cure your perceived problem.

It is crucial in motorsports to create a good handling balance.

Creating a Game Plan

Any plan is better than no plan at all. Take the time to create a game plan for each event, beginning with your realistic objectives, maintenance schedules, testing, and strategy. And remember that part of a good game plan is the flexibility to alter the plan as needed. Usually, no plan equals no result.

Determining Exactly Where the Problem Begins

A handling problem can occur anywhere on the track. Is it corner entry, midturn, corner exit; does it happen everywhere? If a problem occurs in one place, does it result in a different problem someplace else? The classic example of this is corner entry understeer that a driver overcompensates for at the exit of the corner, creating an oversteer condition. The driver says the car is oversteering, but the real problem is the corner entry push. Adjusting for the oversteer will make the problem worse.

Having a Suspension Bind

Suspension binds create an inconsistent handling situation. If a bind is present, it is just about impossible to tune the suspension. If the car does not respond the way you think it should to changes, check for bind in the suspension. And checking for binds should be

This Lexus Grand-Am Cup racecar is showing a perfect handling balance. Much testing and tuning was required to reach that point.

Testing braking performance is part of the whole picture when tuning a car for optimum handling performance. *Jeff Cheechov*

Whether a race team, aftermarket parts company, tuner, or individual, the tires are the key to performance and tire temperatures offer the most useful information. *Rick Herrick*

Aerodynamic downforce can be altered at the front by changing the shape or height of the front air dam. This will change the high-speed handling balance even on a car like this VW Rabbit GTi Cup racer.

too stiff, especially the shock valving, it is difficult for the driver to feel what the chassis is doing. The car reacts too quickly for the driver to sense what is occurring. Softer springs and shocks, while slower for the experienced driver, may be faster for the inexperienced driver.

Making Corner Weight Adjustments at One Corner Only

To adjust the corner weight percentage, you must change the frame height. Suspension geometry is designed to work best at a certain frame height. Changing the frame height can alter the suspension geometry in a negative manner, especially if you make one big change at one corner. The trick is to make small changes at all four corners. Instead of putting a turn in the right front, put a quarter turn in the right front and left rear, and take a quarter turn out of the left front and right rear.

Curing Handling Problems with One Element

Any handling problem can be changed by adjusting several different parts on a car: the wheels, tires, shocks, springs, antiroll bars, differential, and so on. People will try to cure a problem by using what they know best, but you must consider all variables. Look at the entire system as a whole, then make incremental changes that suit the system best and offer the most favorable compromise.

Making More than One Change at a Time

Even though you want to consider all angles, it is always best to make only one change at a time. Making more than one change makes it difficult to determine what resulted from each alteration. One change may have improved some aspect of handling while the other did the opposite.

Moving Too Far Away from Recommended Ride Heights

This can cause binding in the suspension or, at a minimum, cause undesirable suspension geometry.

part of your routine setup process. The control arms, struts, antiroll bars, panhard bars, and tie rods must freely move.

Detecting a Dead Shock

A bad shock can be difficult to feel. Check the shocks if you cannot get the chassis tuned effectively. Feel for dead spots or lack of resistance in both rebound and compression.

An Overly Aggressive Setup

Often, the fastest setup for a given car is too aggressive for a driver without some experience. When the suspension is

Inaccurate Measurements

As bad as not keeping records in the first place is recording inaccurate measurements. Don't waste your dutifully invested measurement time by recording the information so haphazardly you can't read or keep track of it to your advantage.

Inconsistent Fuel Load

Changing fuel load will always be a setup and tuning problem. As fuel is burned off, and its weight removed from the vehicle, handling will change. If you do not tune at a constant fuel load, your data will be inaccurate and the results misleading. No more than a 2-gallon fluctuation is acceptable. One gallon is a better mark.

Crew/Driver Communications

If the crew or driver is not sure of the concepts of tuning and clear about the language, all sorts of problems can occur. Sit down together at the track, a coffee shop, or someone's living room (with the television off!) and talk about tuning and handling concepts until everyone is on the same page. Chances are everyone can pick up a few insights from such a discussion.

Overdriving the Vehicle

If a driver is overdriving the track or setup, most of the data, whether from the driver or tire temperatures, will be less than accurate. Overdriving not only abuses the tires but also masks real handling problems.

Adjustable antiroll bars allow quick, easy, and accurate tuning of roll couple distribution and, therefore, handling balance.

Making Too Big of a Change

If a change is too big, you can cause a handling problem that is worse than the one you already have. On the other hand, a change too small can be difficult to detect by the driver or on the stopwatch. Big changes would be more than two numbers on shock valving, more than 15 percent in spring or bar rate, or more than 1/4 inch in ride height.

Understanding the Whole System

Understanding the whole system is very important. The key is to understand how any change affects the tire contact load and traction. Always thinking in terms of tire contact patch load and traction will help you focus on making the best change possible for the situation.

Coping with Changing Track Conditions

Track conditions constantly change. The car may get faster during the day even though the lap times are slower. The track may be slowing even faster than the car is getting faster. If in doubt, return to the starting setup to see how the track has changed.

Running Old Tires

At some point, tires get too hard to be fast. Even if the tread surface looks good, an old, hard tire can't catch new, softer ones, all other things being equal.

How to Cure Driver-Induced Handling Problems

The driver is often the culprit behind handling problems, a situation that can be difficult to detect and correct for two reasons. First, handling problems can be easily masked since several different scenarios can be the cause for a given problem. Second, it can be difficult for drivers to have the insight and honesty needed to look within for the problem. It takes courage and commitment to confront yourself and your ego to seek the truth. There are several clues to help determine whether the car or the driver is the root of the problem.

- If the problem is inconsistent, it is most likely driver-induced.
- If a problem occurs at every similar type of turn, it is most likely, but not always, setup related.
- On road courses, if a problem occurs on either left or right turns only, it is likely setup related.
- If the problem occurs at one turn only or one segment of a turn, it is likely driver-induced.

There are hundreds of possible handling scenarios and even more ways to change them. By focusing on what is happening at the tire contact patch, you have the best chance to effect a change that improves performance. And remember that the driver is one of the vehicle systems that affects handling. Always consider what the driver does with the controls as one of the potential sources for a problem as well as one of the possible cures.

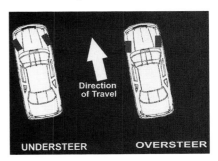

This illustration shows the difference between understeer and oversteer.

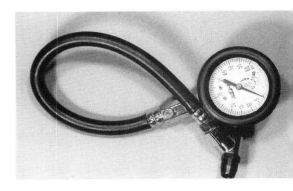

A good tire pressure gauge is a critical component in your tuning toolbox.

Chapter Thirteen
Tuning with Shocks

In the middle of a race, you are running just behind the race leader. He is pulling away slightly, and the place on the race track where he seems to gain is going into the corners under braking. You're driving in just as deep as you can, but the leader is able to drive in a half-car-length deeper. If you go in that hard you pick up a push. The car is great everywhere else, and you can run with the leader. Your cars are identical and on the same tires, so what could his advantage be? It's a frustrating race, even though you finish second, because you just can't quite run with the leader.

This scenario could be improved by making a shock change. The trick is defining the problem, determining where it happens, and making the best choice to help cure the problem. A key word here is *problem*. Shocks really don't cure problems, but they can be great for making small improvements in handling in specific parts of the track or in a corner. *Shocks can be used to fine-tune the handling balance of a racecar during transitions.* Shocks will not cure a big handling problem, though they can cause handling

On the highway, shock tuning is important to find the balance between performance and ride comfort. *James Brown*

The shock absorbers play a major role in transient handling response as shown on this slalom course. *Rick Herrick*

problems if they are bent, bind, or are way too stiff or soft.

Shocks affect how fast weight is transferred. This changes the tire loading while the shock is still moving in either bump or rebound travel.

How Shocks Affect Handling

The shock controls how fast weight is transferred. This affects the load on a tire and can change the handling balance while weight is being transferred. Once all weight has been transferred, the shock no longer influences handling. Since weight is almost always being transferred, the shocks are almost always affecting handling balance.

In general, rebound damping controls how fast weight leaves a tire, while bump controls how fast weight goes onto a tire. Stiffer valving causes a shock to react and the load to change more quickly; softer valving slows shock reaction and weight transfer. Stiffer rebound valving gets the load off a tire more quickly and onto the diagonally opposite tire faster going into or out of a corner. Stiffer bump valving gets the load onto that tire faster. If all the valving, both bump and rebound at all four corners, is changed equally, the effect on handling balance is minimal. If only bump or rebound is changed, or only one end or

Corner entry handling problems can be cured with shocks if the problems are small. Often corner entry problems are unnoticed when the driver overcorrects and creates a problem on the exit as a result. The problem must be isolated to be cured effectively.

Shocks have less of an effect in midcorner, but can still help get a better handling balance and make the car quicker and easier to drive through the middle.

corner (or diagonal corners) is changed, then there is an effect.

In road racing or autocrossing, when going into a corner, as long as the driver is moving (as opposed to holding stationary) either the steering wheel or the brake pedal, the shock has an influence on tire loading. Braking causes weight to transfer forward, compressing the front suspension and shocks, extending the rear suspension and shocks. When cornering, the weight transfers from the inside to the outside, extending the inside suspension and shocks while compressing the outside suspension and shocks. When both braking and cornering take place, as they nearly always do going into a turn, both effects occur. In a left turn, the right front, which is compressing both from roll and pitch, and the left rear, which is extending from both factors, are moving the most and will have the biggest influence. The left front and right rear are receiving the opposite movement from roll and pitch, reducing their influence.

Midcorner, where the longitudinal forces (braking and acceleration) are small and lateral forces (cornering) are highest, all of the shocks have an influence; but shock travel is very small and this reduces the influence.

At the exit, we basically undo what happened going into a corner. Under acceleration, the rear shocks go into compression and the fronts into rebound. As cornering is reduced, the inside shocks go into compression and the outside shocks into rebound. Exiting a left turn, the left rear and right front move the most since those shocks have forces working in the same direction (roll force helps decompress the right front shock; acceleration pitch helps the left rear shock return from rebound), while the left front and right rear have opposing forces. Do not take this to mean that the left front and right rear shocks do not influence handling in a left turn. *They do.* The effect is just a little less. And everything reverses in a right-hand turn, so all four shocks have a big influence.

If you are drag racing on a front-driver you want to keep weight on the front tires as long as possible. On a rear-driver, you want weight to transfer to the rear as quickly as possible. If the alignment, static weight distribution, and spring/bar rates are optimized, then shocks can be used to improve starting-line launch acceleration. On the front-driver, stiffer front rebound will hold the weight on the front a little longer and softer rear bump will delay weight transfer slightly. On a rear-drive car, stiffer rear bump and stiffer front rebound will get weight to the rear more quickly. While not a major factor, it can be worth a tenth or so on the launch.

Let's go back to the earlier example. A slight push going into the corners keeps the driver from braking as late as the other car. Keep in mind, this is a very slight push. The car has a good basic setup and is fast. The car ahead is about 1/10th of second a lap faster. Shocks can be very helpful in this situation.

Under hard braking and some cornering in a left turn, the right front is the heaviest-loaded tire on most cars. A push means the front tires are exceed-ing optimum traction limits. We need a little more traction on the front, and a little less on the rear. A big change could make the car loose going into the turns. Changing the springs or antiroll bar could erode the perfect balance of the car on the exit; even a shock change could do that.

Here is a case where going to the left rear or right front would have an effect. Stiffer rebound on the left rear or left front, or stiffer bump on the right front, will get weight off the rear and onto the right front more quickly. The left front is the least useful change, since that will take load off the left front more quickly, slightly reducing traction there. The right front is good change, but the best is the left rear rebound.

The left rear in many if not most cases has more travel in this situation than any other shock, so it is a good change to make, since it is likely to be most effective. Of course, you'll be turning right at some point, so the right rear shock in rebound will affect right turns the most. You may or may not end up with the same rebound valving on the left versus right rear shock, but

Shocks can help cure corner exit handling problems, but often the driver is causing a problem by accelerating too hard too soon. The shocks can help in this situation, but probably won't cure the problem. *Bob Schroeder*

most likely, the pairs will be the same valving or settings.

Back to the left-turn example. A stiffer shock on the left rear will help the entry push problem. Let's say we go one click, or number, stiffer in both bump and rebound. We want the stiffer rebound, but what will the stiffer bump valving on the left rear do to the handling? If it helps going in it will likely loosen the car on the exit. Since the exit is more important than the entry for faster lap times, this may not be such a good change.

In most cases where the car is really good except for one spot in a corner, the best change is using an adjustable shock where at least rebound settings can be changed, or use a split-valve shock. You could also have a shock manufacturer custom-valve a shock for you. In our example, going up one click or one valving number increases the rebound valving while the bump valving remains the same. This cures the entry push without changing the balance in midturn or on the exit. But if the push were bigger, this change may help a little, but would not cure the problem. Look somewhere else in this case.

Let's look at one more example. In this case, the car is loose on exit. Again a shock change will only help if the car is really close to begin with. And here, the problem could be caused by the driver spinning the rear tires under acceleration. This is especially likely on a slow corner. A shock change will help a little here, but will not cure the problem. In a left turn, we could decrease the left rear bump or decrease the right front rebound. Decreasing bump stiffness at one corner has a similar affect as increasing rebound travel at the opposite end. The opposite is also true. When only rebound is adjustable, that's what you change, but you keep in mind that changing rebound damping from

Shocks play a big role in transitions. Stiff low-speed valving in both bump and rebound can help make the transitions from left to right (or right to left) occur more quickly. What may be great for a road racing application may be too soft for an autocross situation. The abrupt transitions found on an autocross course are rare on a road course. *Jeff Donker*

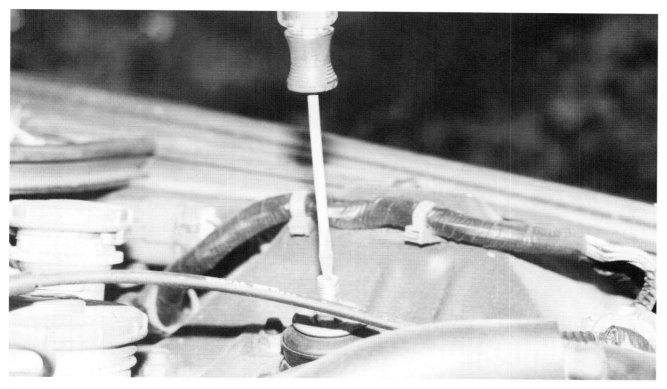

Externally adjustable shock valving allows quick adjustments and is a nice touch for multi-use vehicles.

one situation can have a different, even undesirable, effect in another situation. It lets the weight get off that corner faster, which would help the most, but the left rear bump reduction would be nearly as good. Again, adjustable shocks or split-valve shocks will help here. For other scenarios, see the accompanying chart.

Tuning for Bumps

A really bumpy track may require softer shocks overall, especially in rebound. If one bump is upsetting the balance of the car in one or two places on the track, a change would help there but may hurt everywhere else. Here you must make a compromise.

Baseline Shocks

In 95 percent of all cases, the baseline shocks should be the ones recommended by your shock manufacturer for the type of car and track you're running. Extremely bumpy tracks may

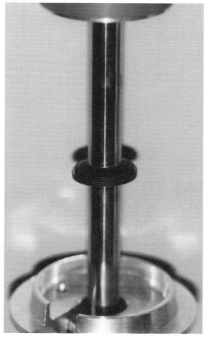

Shock bump travel, which can be measured with the rubber grommet on the shaft, is a good indicator of how bumpy the surface is and what possible high and medium shaft speed valving should be.

This Progress coil-over shock can be revalved in both bump and rebound and for various shaft speeds in order to fine-tune transient handling balance.

require a change to softer shocks if the car skates over the bumps or feels unstable. Many racers make the mistake of going too far away from the baseline setup and end up with an unworkable setup on the car.

When to Tune with Shocks

The following are some important criteria when tuning with shocks that could help make your car faster:

- Each tire contact patch *must* be optimized. Camber, caster, tire pressure, and toe must be right before tuning with shocks. If these aren't right, you're chasing your tail and wasting time.
- Static weights and cross-weight percentages must be close to optimum.
- Make sure that there are absolutely no binds in the suspension.
- Define where the problem occurs. Often a corner exit problem is a corner entry problem not recognized by the driver. A driver can easily overcompensate for corner entry understeer, causing an oversteer condition on exit.
- The handling problem must be small. The car should already be fast. Don't expect more than a .2- to .4-second improvement in lap

times, de-pending on the nature of the times.
- It takes a skilled driver who is consistent and sensitive to changes to really tune with shocks. New drivers should spend a test day making shock changes to the car to see what they do. This experience is extremely important to wring the last little

bit of performance out of the car.
- Make small changes. Going up two numbers, or two clicks, on adjustable shocks is a big change. And only change one corner or one end of the car at a time when tuning with shocks.
- Consult with the shock absorber manufacturer technical representatives for guidance.

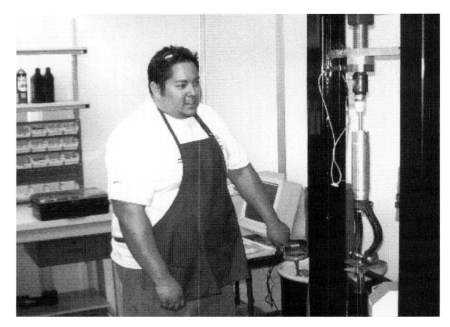

A shock dyno like this one at the Progress Group is an invaluable tool for determining the damping characteristics of a shock. This is necessary for street applications to ensure good ride as well as performance, but it is a must for motorsports applications. *Progress Group*

SHOCKS Increase or decrease damping; make only one change. **Bold is best change.**	RF BUMP	RF REBOUND	LF BUMP	LF REBOUND	RR BUMP	RR REBOUND	LR BUMP	LR REBOUND
CORNER ENTRY PUSH	decrease			increase				increase
MID-CORNER PUSH				**increase**				
CORNER EXIT PUSH		**increase**					increase	
CORNER ENTRY LOOSE		increase						decrease
MID-CORNER LOOSE				**decrease**	decrease			
CORNER EXIT LOOSE		**decrease**					decrease	

This chart is a guide for shock changes to improve handling. *Push* refers to understeer and *loose* refers to oversteer. Remember that shocks should only be used for tuning when the car is already close to perfect. Shocks can be used for fine-tuning specific problems when properly identified at specific points in a turn.

It takes a lot of parts to assemble custom-valved shocks at the Progress Group. *Progress Group*

Shocks are clearly a very valuable tuning tool on a racecar. Understanding what a shock can do is important. Getting the desired results takes effort and skill. Don't expect too much, get a good basic setup on your car, and then making small shock changes can pay big dividends.

This is a cutaway of a Progress Group Competition coil-over. This shock allows re-valving by the racer with a kit from Progress. This makes fine-tuning shocks less expensive than when using externally adjustable units. *Progress Group*

Chapter Fourteen
Motorsports

It's Sunday afternoon. You just finished watching a CART race, where a Honda-powered car won. Now you're watching a British Touring Car race and a Honda Accord won! Your brand-new V-6 Accord is sitting in the driveway, dressed with 17-inch wheels and sticky tires, an aero kit, and high-performance suspension, but with no place to go. You'd really love to try your ride at the limit, but the traffic is too heavy and the winding country roads are just too dangerous. It's time to tape those races on the tube and slide behind the wheel for some real hands-on action.

While I certainly consider myself to be a world champion–caliber couch pilot, it's way more fun to power slide the real thing through a series of corners. And there are several ways you can do that, from mild to wild, and many are surprisingly inexpensive. Different clubs and types of events are available to suit individual needs, desires, and goals. Here's an overview.

Drag Racing

One of the easiest forms of motorsport to jump into is drag racing.

Participation in motorsports is exciting at all levels. This Nissan Super Touring car in the British Touring Car Championship is the pinnacle of stock platform road racing.

Street legal drag racing is a great way to participate in motorsports regardless of the type of car or its modifications. *Hotchkis Tuning*

The process is simple to understand, procedures are easy, and the skills required to have fun are minimal. Car setup is unnecessary for entry-level stock classes.

On the one hand, drag racing at the entry level is cheap. On the other, it can cost $50,000 to build a 10-second quarter-mile machine. The fun level of quarter mile runs is high, but the track time is minimal and often the wait between runs is very long. No license beyond a driver's license is needed to compete, and entry fees are small.

Autocross/Solo II

Here is another form of the sport that is very easy to get involved in. An autocross or Solo II is a mini-road-course set up most often in a parking lot with orange traffic cones. Speeds are low, and while sticky tires will make your ride faster, you don't need them to give autocrossing a try. If you get serious about competing in a prepared class, car modifications to your daily driver can range up to several thousand dollars, but very limited modifications

are allowed in the stock classes. Runs last about a minute and you normally get three or four in an afternoon. Expect to spend a couple of hours working the course while other classes compete. It's all part of the fun.

Autocrossing requires no special license, but the extreme left and right turns do require considerable skill to master. Entry fees are low, and even if you pop for a set of sticky race-compound tires, they will last you many events. Autocrossing provides a fun,

exciting, and challenging element of the sport for low cost and little time commitment.

Time Trials/Track Day

The time trial may offer the most bang for the buck. A time trial is an event on a road course with no wheel-to-wheel competition. While you are on the track with other cars, passing is allowed only on designated long straights. You must keep minimum distances between cars and car-to-car contact is strictly prohibited. You can easily reach racing speeds, but the damage and crash risk is greatly reduced compared to road racing. Events range from one to two days and typical track time is more than one hour each day.

Many groups around the country run time trials, so finding an event is easy. Track groups are run based on experience and car performance, so your Honda Civic will not be on the track with a race-prepped NSX. Many clubs have organized classes and lap times are taken with the fast time in class winning a trophy. And nearly every club or time trial group offers instruction from experienced racers. These instructors often work for racing schools, and they usually know their stuff.

Any kind of car is allowed, and modifications are no problem. Cars are teched prior to events, and a helmet is required along with a functional driver restraint. And some groups allow

Autocrossing allows the driver to reach handling limits at low speed and in a safe environment.

Any type of car can participate in autocrossing. *Bob Schroeder*

fun, challenging, and easy. Usually run by local car clubs, these events require no special driving skills or car setup techniques. Speed is not a factor as they are run on public roads with normal traffic, and all traffic laws must be obeyed. This type of rally focuses on the driver's and navigator's ability to read and follow often misleading route instructions.

Navigation rallies, which are also called time-speed-distance rallies, require a very precise ability where the driver and navigator must cover a specific section of the route in an exact time. Penalty points are given for every second of variation from the specified time. Covering a 35-minute segment of public roads and hitting the checkpoint at the exact second is a huge challenge. When you leave a checkpoint, your start time is recorded, and the same occurs when you reach the next checkpoint. In between you follow a series of instructions (not a road map) to get from one checkpoint to the next. Not so easy. In a single evening event with five stages, the overall winner is often within 10 seconds of the minimum time. Any kind of car will work and minimal equipment is needed for this type of event.

Pro Rally is an SCCA class based on top-level rallying throughout the world. While this type of rally is also a time-speed-distance event, here many of the stages are on closed highways and forest roads and the allotted time for stages requires flat-out driving. In the United States, SCCA Pro rallies are run mostly on dirt forest roads and require fully prepared cars. This level of rallying is tremendous fun but is costly and time-consuming.

passengers, which adds an interesting element to the fun. Entry costs are low for the track time, tire wear is fairly high, and you can expect to accelerate the wear and tear on your machine, especially brakes, but it is hard to find a more fun way to play.

Rallying

Rallying comes in several flavors, ranging from a Friday- or Saturday-night skill/gimmick rally or navigation rally to full-blown Pro Rallies with fully prepared rally cars and stiff competition. Skill/gimmick rallies are

Rallycross

Rallycross is somewhat rare in the United States. A rallycross is simply an autocross on dirt or gravel. A tight, pylon course laid out on dirt requires good car control and some chassis setup, but otherwise nothing special.

Rallysprint

A rallysprint is also on dirt or a combined dirt/asphalt course, but it's a wheel-to-wheel event-like road racing. This is even rarer in the United States, but it's available in some regions. Like road racing, rallysprint is more costly and time-consuming than rallycross.

Road Racing

If you like intensity, adrenaline, and a major test of skill, road racing is the way to fly. Nothing compares to the challenge presented by competing against a group of equally intense racers on a twisting, high-speed road circuit. It just doesn't get any better.

To go road racing requires a license, a car with the required safety equipment, and a budget ranging from a few hundred dollars a race to several million if racing in the CART Champ Car series is your cup of tea. At the club level, road racing, while not cheap, is affordable and not as difficult as many think. Getting involved is relatively easy. On a national level, the Sports Car Club of America has regions throughout the country and classes for most cars. Other clubs, including the National Auto Sport Association (which is expanding into several areas of the country) and the Racecar Club of America (in the East), conduct races on a regional level.

Racing costs involve entry fees ranging from $200 to 300 for a weekend, maintenance, and tires. For the stock classes, a set of tires costs between $300 and $500, and a set will last for three to seven weekends of racing. At the entry level, our GTi Cup VW Rabbit project car cost from $4,000 to $6,000 fully prepared. Without full safety equipment, your daily driver would not pass tech inspection for road racing like it would for a time trial. Not counting travel expenses, you can race for as little as $400 to $500 per weekend. While

continued on page 132

Track days are a great way to test your driving skill and your car's performance at speed in a safe, exciting atmosphere. Track days usually require only basic car safety equipment and inspection. Drivers must wear approved helmets. *Hotchkis Tuning*

One of the most exciting and challenging forms of motorsports is rallying. From the World Rally Championship in which this Subaru WRX competes to local SCCA club events, rallying offers an extreme driving and performance challenge. *Subaru USA*

Speed trials at places like Bonneville and El Mirage are becoming increasingly popular. Good handling is just as important at these events as in any other form of motorsports. *Progress Group*

Racing Associations

Arizona Sports Racing Association
602-844-9677
Competition Motorsports Association
918-583-1134
Eastern Motor Racing Association
516-728-5111
Midwestern Council of Sports Car Clubs
708-359-0204
National Auto Sport Association (NASA)
888-946-6272
Racecar Club of America (RCCA)
914-576-7222
Sports Car Club of America (SCCA)
303-779-6622

Regional Sports Car Clubs

Akron Sports Car Club
216-833-3189
Autocrossers, Inc.
301-461-5743
CAL Club Autocross
909-947-0644
CAL Poly Sports Car Club
805-773-0331
Connecticut Autocross and Rally Team
203-729-7164

Council of Motorsports Clubs-
Rocky Mountains
970-523-1669
Equipe Rapide
972-394-2929
Fairfield County Sports Car Club
203-926-8552
Highlands Sports Car Club
704-891-8855
North Hills Sports Car Club
412-486-9196
Porsche Owners Club
714-779-8695
Southern California Council of Sports
Car Clubs
818-249-5761
Tarheel Sports Car Club
919-662-7502
Tidewater Sports Car Club
804-421-3041
Trans Louisiana Autocross
Championship
504-467-8910
Triad Sports Car Club
910-954-9575
Virginia Motor Sport Club
804-320-7822

Racing Schools

Bob Bondurant School of
High-Performance Driving
800-842-7223
Bridgestone Winter Driving School
800-949-7543
Car Guys
800-800-4897
Mid-Ohio School
614-793-4615
PDA School
201-773-4800
Pit Arresi Racing School
503-285-4449
Road Atlanta School
770-967-6143
Bertil Roos Grand Prix Racing School
717-646-7227
Russell Racing School
707-939-7600
Skip Barber Racing School
800-221-1131
Trackmasters
716-624-5520
Trackspeed
813-249-0328

	Import Drag Racing	Autocross/ Solo II	Rallying	Time Trials	Road Racing	Racing Schools
Ease of Participation	easy	more difficult	more difficult	more difficult	difficult	easy
Safety	very safe	very safe	somewhat dangerous (public roads)	safe	somewhat dangerous (wheel-to-wheel racing)	safe
Vehicle wear & tear	moderate	moderate	moderate to high	moderate	moderately high	none
Cost to participate	low	low	moderate to high	moderate	moderate to high	moderate to high
Track time	seconds/day	minutes/day	hours/event	1+ hours/ day	1+ hours/ day	1 to 3 hours/ day
Maintenance cost	moderate	moderate	moderate to high	moderate to high	moderate to high	none
Maintenance time	moderate	moderate	moderate to high	moderate to high	moderate to high	none
Fun for investment	moderate	moderate	moderate to high	high	high	moderate to high
Accessibility	good	excellent	weak	good	good	good
Potential car damage	low	very low	high	moderate	high	none
Car preparation cost	zero to very high	low	zero to high	moderate	high	none

Groups like the Sports Car Club of America, National Auto Sport Association, Touring Car Club, Racecar Club of America, Porsche Owners Club, BMW Car Club of America, and many others offer opportunities to go road racing.

Audi Quattro Challenge

A unique event for Audi owners, the Audi Quattro Challenge provides a venue for owners to take their cars to the limit in a very safe and exciting environment. Held at California Speedway and Nazareth Speedway in Pennsylvania, the Quattro Challenge provided four driving events, three of which were in the participants' own cars. An autocross course provided timed runs, a wet-and-dry accident-avoidance course taught drivers car control under extreme conditions, a wet handling course offered the biggest driving challenge, and participants drove a selection of Audis on a road course. The S4 Avant and sedan were shod with Pirelli P Zero C DOT legal race compound tires, adding to the traction as well as the challenge. The event was a sellout, extremely well organized and everyone experienced the great features of their own Audis as well as the benefits of the new models. Most of the participants were first-timers to motorsports events. This is the perfect way to get your feet wet in motorsports activities in a safe, friendly, and exciting environment. Other manufacturers will certainly follow the lead set by Audi by conducting similar events for customers. For more information on the Audi Quattro Challenge, see www.myaudi.com. Other events are available for all types of cars in the club listing elsewhere in this chapter.

An instructor at the Audi Quattro Challenge directs a participant on the autocross course.

Participants at the Audi Quattro Challenge could test new TTs, the AllRoad, and the new 2002 A4 on a twisty course while waiting for a turn on the accident avoidance course.

The dry portion of the accident avoidance course allowed drivers to reach the limits of traction in an abrupt maneuver situation but with nothing to hit.

Street Stock Endurance road racing is very popular. Races are about three hours long, and two or more drivers share the ride. This event in Arizona was run by Grand Am Racing.

SCCA Production classes allow the most modifications for production-based cars. *Progress Group*

The FastLane Racing School uses Toyota Celicas from the Long Beach Grand Prix Celebrity race. *Fastlane Racing School*

Continued from page 127

crashes occur, they are rare in club racing, and injuries are even more unusual. Considering the action, excitement, fun, and challenge, the cost of road racing is relatively small.

Racing Schools

The best way to get your feet wet in autosports is by attending a racing school. They usually provide everything you need, including the car. In addition to the instruction provided, you will have the chance to find out how much you enjoy the activity before you invest in any equipment. And the school itself is fun and cost-effective. When selecting a school, find out about the track time, damage liability, and prices before you register or make travel plans. Some comparison shopping can save you a lot of money and aggravation.

Section II
Project Cars

This section of *High-Performance Handling Handbook* contains several project cars. A wide range of vehicles and modifications is covered in this section. While space does not permit detailed buildups and how-to procedures, you will get a sense of what can be accomplished with certain types of products, modifications, and tuning. The vehicles range from very mild modifications (wheel and tires only) to full-blown racecars.

In every case, the products used on these vehicles come from manufacturers making quality products. The one thing each company shares is engineering and testing. It is not possible to create good suspension components, wheels, and tires without solid engineering and testing. Certainly there are other companies creating products

with quality engineering, testing, and materials, but I have had solid relationships with these companies, in some cases for more than a decade. I know they do it right.

In each case, these cars were tested and, in most cases, tuned by me. Each vehicle was built for a specific purpose with improved handling performance always one of the primary goals. In each case, those goals were met. The idea is to help you understand what is possible and what it takes to reach a certain goal. You can do this with virtually any vehicle, limited only by parts availability, imagination, and resources. You do not need the same type of vehicle used here.

If you decide to modify a vehicle, understand that the work you are undertaking requires a certain level of

skill and appropriate equipment. Most of the tasks are accomplished with basic mechanical skills and hand tools. Replacing springs should be done by a professional due to the high preload on the springs. A spring compressor must be used and knowing how is crucial.

Never undertake mechanical work without a thorough knowledge of the skills needed and the proper procedures. If fabrication is needed, especially welding, pay a professional to do the work. A failed weld on a suspension component can mean an ugly situation on the road or the track. Welding is required on roll cages, and your life depends on the quality of the workmanship. Use a reputable—preferably a certified—welder for any welding fabrication.

Chapter Fifteen
Audi Project Car

Prior to the modifications, the Avant performed exceptionally well on mountain roads.

Audi A4 Avant Quattro Street Car

With a car starting at the level of an Audi A4 Quattro Avant, it's difficult to imagine making significant improvements to the handling. The A4's single weakness, and it's a moderate one, is the original tire selection. The Dunlop SP Sport rubber is a very good compromise for most conditions that Audi owners may experience. They are good in the wet and are especially good on windy mountain and canyon roads, but provide less than ideal performance in the snow. Testing different

tires for different uses, based on the versatility of A4 Quattro, made sense to us, so that is just what we did. Finding the optimum tires for different conditions would allow the Audi to shine.

Our project A4 Quattro Avant is equipped with the 190-horsepower 2.8-liter V-6 engine, Tiptronic automatic transmission, and the optional sport suspension package. Bone stock, the car is a joy to drive. Handling is near neutral with reasonable grip. This car is driven in a wide variety of conditions, including snow and occasional motorsports events,

such as the Audi Quattro Challenge (see chapter 14, Motorsports).

Three specific conditions require three different types of tires. First, for performance driving and motorsports events, an ultra-high-performance tire is the most desirable. Next, daily driving on mostly dry roads, some rural, some interstate, and some around town, requires a slightly more conservative tire that did not adversely affect ride comfort or noise levels. And finally, a good snow tire for winter driving conditions would be nice.

The H & R Coil-over kit features more aggressive shock valving and stiffer springs as well as adjustable ride height. The design of the Audi suspension allows for easy installation of the H & R Coil-overs. The spring/shock unit is attached to a cast-aluminum upper mounting plate, and you can remove it from the car without compressing the spring. A spring compressor is needed to remove the spring from the plate after removal from the car. The H & R unit uses the existing mounts and bolts in perfectly. Spring adjustment is a breeze with the spanner wrenches provided with the kit.

On the suspension side, the sport package on the Avant is fairly aggressive, but the ride height, like the tire choice, is a compromise: too high for high-performance situations and a little too low for good ground clearance in winter driving conditions. The compromise is actually a good one, but it is still a compromise.

The excellent geometry of the A4 lends itself to high-performance applications, but the body roll is a little excessive, and lowering the car would improve dry handling. Changing springs and shocks is a four-hour task (see chapter 2 for details). Doing that several times a year for differing conditions and uses would be impractical. Spending a half-hour to change wheels and tires and adjust ride height is acceptable.

To accomplish this, H & R Springs' Roland Graf suggested a set of its coil-overs for the S4 Avant. H & R Springs'

A4 package is just slightly more aggressive than the factory optional sport suspension package on the car, and considering the performance applications for this project, the more aggressive S4 package would work well. The adjustable spring perches on the H & R Springs coil-overs allow ride height adjustments over about a 4-inch range. You can lower by more than 2-1/2 inches and raise the car by nearly 1-1/2 inches above stock.

This was the perfect solution to meet the project goals, as long as the ride quality was not destroyed, since most of the driving with this car is around town and on interstates.

Unlike most coil-over systems, H & R Springs coil-overs use hard rubber bushings where the units attach to the chassis and the suspension. While sacrificing some responsiveness, these hard rubber bushings also isolate some road noise, vibration, and ride harshness. They have proven to be an excellent compromise. First, the stiffer springs and lower ride height reduce body roll, which helps keep the tire contact patches on the road surface more uniformly. Second, the stiffer shocks improve transient handling response, but medium- and high-speed valving are fairly soft, allowing good control over bumpy surfaces and good ride quality. In fact, the combination of stiffer springs and shocks does not affect ride comfort significantly. The car maintains its very comfortable feel

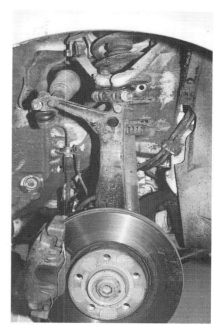

The stock suspension on the Audi A4 Avant Quattro project uses a coil-over shock/spring design. The A4 was equipped with the Sport Suspension package as shown here.

and interior noise level, depending on the tires being used.

Which brings us to the next part of the story—tires.

The stock Dunlops are a good compromise between dry traction and wet conditions. But for performance driving situations such as the occasional motorsports event, pushing the performance envelope was a must. For this we selected the BFG g-Force T/A KD max ultra-high-performance tire. The

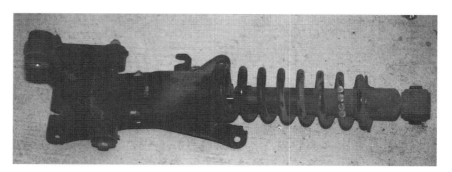

The stock rear spring/shock unit requires the removal of one upper control arm bolt, one lower shock mount bolt, and four bracket bolts. The spring is compressed and the upper shock bolt removed. The H & R coil-over unit is a perfect bolt-in replacement.

The modifications made to the Audi A4 Quattro turned an exceptional handling car into a cornering rocket on both the track and the road. Corner exit is flat with the addition of the H & R Springs coilover kit.

The H & R Coil-over unit installed in the rear allows easy ride height adjustments. The shock mounts are hard rubber bushings that isolate road noise and vibration, making the H & R system quiet and smooth as well as much more aggressive on the handling side.

size is also pushing the envelope with a 225/40 ZR18, about as large as the stock fender well can accommodate.

The wheel selection was an 18.-x 8.5-inch Zender Monza from Autotech Sport Tuning. Not only beautiful, these wheels are very strong and fairly lightweight for a one-piece alloy. With a 35-millimeter offset, the wheel fit perfectly with the BFGs.

Ride height was finally set at 1.5 inches lower than stock with this setup for motorsports activities. Any lower would cause problems over steep drives and serious potholes. Even this ride height requires care when approaching steep driveways in order to avoid scraping the underside of the chassis.

Four characteristics of the g-Force T/A KD tires are apparent immediately. First is the increased grip. Cornering speeds are much higher and stopping distances are reduced. Second, standing-start acceleration is slightly

reduced, due to the increased weight of the much larger wheel/tire combo. Third, road noise is much louder, a characteristic of most max performance tires. Finally, the ride is much harsher. The very low sidewall profile and stiff construction characteristics account for this.

But the grip is worth it most of the time. These tires were tested at the Audi Quattro Challenge at California Speedway, and they have very high levels of grip. But, most important, they are totally predictable, very forgiving, and response is nearly instantaneous. Overall, they are excellent performers.

Two of the exercises at the Challenge were in the wet. While no max performance tire is at its best in the wet, the level of wet traction was very surprising, being much higher than anticipated. And the tire maintained its good manners in the wet, another plus for this tire.

While these tires would be more prone to aquaplaning over standing puddles of water like any tire in this category, when the road is damp or wet, but not flooded, these tires work as well anything. But forget using them in winter driving conditions. Too wide and too low of a void ratio for adverse weather.

I've spent many test hours on high-performance BFG tires, and I have always loved driving on them. With high grip, consistent feel at the limit, and no surprises, they have always been fast, predictable, forgiving, and responsive. The g-Force T/A KD is even better than its predecessors.

Next, the Yokohama AVS Sport max performance tire was tried. We wanted to test a plus-one combo so we used a 215/45 ZR17 tire on 17x7.5-inch wheels. This is a very aggressive tire like the g-Force KD, but is slightly (1/4 inch) narrower and the sidewall is taller. Grip is nearly the same. It would be impossible to tell the difference without considerable A-B testing. Ride is better, but response to steering inputs is slightly slower. All of these characteristics are predictable. So is the fact that the tire is a dream to drive on.

Like BFGs, I have many test hours on Yokohama tires, and I love the feel of them. They are very responsive to driver steering inputs. If daily driving and some canyon running were all this car would do, this tire would be the perfect compromise.

Trying a stock wheel–size ultra-high-performance tire was next on the agenda. The Yokohama Parada in a 205/45 ZR 16 was the choice. This tire is slightly wider, slightly shorter, and a little stickier than the OE Dunlops. They are quiet, response to steering inputs is very good, and grip levels are more than most drivers will ever use in anything short of a panic situation. If you just wanted a good tire on the stock rim, this tire would be hard to beat.

Finally, we tried a snow tire on the stock wheels. The Toyo Observe in a 205/55 R16 was used on snowy mountain roads. There is nothing more fun than driving in fresh snow (but not ice) with snow tires and the excellent Audi Quattro system.

The Observe is nothing short of phenomenal on the snow. Acceleration, braking, and cornering grip were surprisingly impressive. These tires make driving the car very predicable in circumstances normally considered unpredictable and taxing. Forward traction exiting corners is excellent, and excessive throttle application is easily controlled with a little counter-steering. The car feels completely stable and predictable at small drift angles. Cornering is good and braking performance is confidence-instilling.

Overall, the Toyo Observe gives the already strong Quattro even more grip in the most taxing conditions, especially with the ride height above stock. In the dry, the performance is less impressive, as one would expect. Road noise on the interstate is higher, and grip levels are lower than the orig-

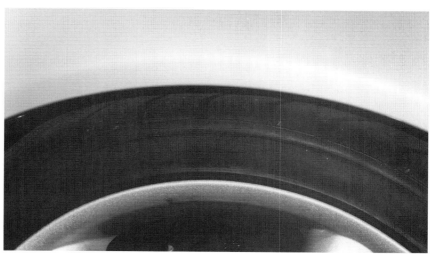

This before- and after-series on the Audi A4 Avant Quattro project shows stock ride height wheel well clearance versus the lowest ride height with the H & R Coil-overs. The tires clear fine at this ride height, but a little more ground clearance is needed for bumps and driveways in daily driving. The H & R Coil-overs allow ride heights greater than stock, which is ideal for off-road driving like rallying or winter conditions in the mountains where snow buildup can require more ground clearance.

inal tires. But overall, the winter compromise is worth the extra grip and high fun factor when the snow falls.

Taking a great car, adding the H & R Springs coil-overs for better handling performance and ride height flexibility, and fitting job-specific wheels and tires proved to bring the absolute best out of the Audi A4 Avant Quattro.

The Toyo Observe snow tires are perfect for winter driving. The BFG

g-Force T/A KD max performance tires are great for driving to the limit at motorsports events. The Yokohama AVS Sports offer a slightly different compromise compared to the BFGs. And the Yokohama Parada ultra-high-performance tires are great on the stock wheels. The alternatives in tires/wheels combined with the the excellent coil-overs make the Avant Quattro like having four different cars, each a great ride.

Chapter Sixteen
Honda Project Cars

The Progress Group Honda del Sol exceeded 1.0 G for its two-way average on the skid pad. *Jeff Cheechov*

1992 Honda Del Sol Tuner Car

The amazing part of the project is that this unassuming little car, fun right off the showroom floor, can be tweaked a little and go around corners better than racecars of three decades ago and keep up with super cars costing over $100,000. Can you imagine the look on a Porsche 911 Turbo owner's face when you keep pace through that long, medium-speed off ramp in a Honda del Sol S?

Getting any car to go around corners with good balance, predictability and comfort in excess of 1.0g cornering force is an engineering feat. Doing that with an inexpensive platform, for not much cash outlay, no fender mods to get more rubber on the road and a good ride is miraculous.

Most of the time, improved handling comes at the cost of a very stiff, usually uncomfortable ride. Not so with the Progress Honda del Sol.

That's not to say the ride is cushy soft, but it is very acceptable, especially considering the performance on those winding roads and freeway ramps. Good spring design and using the right components makes all the difference. And the Progress springs are designed to maintain some ride comfort. That design philosophy has the added benefit of improved cornering performance over bumpy roads. When springs are too stiff, the tire contact

The Progress del Sol was quick, nimble, and sure-footed on the straight-line slalom. *Jeff Cheechov*

Body roll was excessive with the stock suspension. *Jeff Cheechov*

patches easily lose contact with the road over bumps. Considering the condition of modern roads, this is a big plus for any vehicle that will see street duty.

The Progress Sport Spring and antiroll bar package is engineered to provide control over bumps, a reasonable ride and reduced body roll so that the maximum tire contact patch is available for cornering and braking. Progress also selects the best shock absorbers to work with their package. This ensures the best possible control of the springs and the optimum responsiveness when cornering, braking, and accelerating. Combine this with the best wheel/tire package for the application and you have a transformed car. The kinds of numbers generated in our test are not possible without a well-engineered selection of components. The Progress package is just that.

Improving Performance

The stock del Sol is a nice car offering good cornering performance for the buck. But if you really like to drive, the del Sol leaves you wanting more. Adding wheels and tires helps a lot, but the car really needs to be lowered for an aggressive look and improved cornering speed. The Progress springs do both. Add the Tokico Illumina Adjustable shocks and the gain is substantial. The springs alone are too stiff for the stock shocks. Add the front and rear antiroll bars, and the car comes alive in the corners. The tires hook up, and the balance is near perfect with just a hint of throttle on understeer and throttle off oversteer. The car is totally controllable and predictable, and a good driver can really

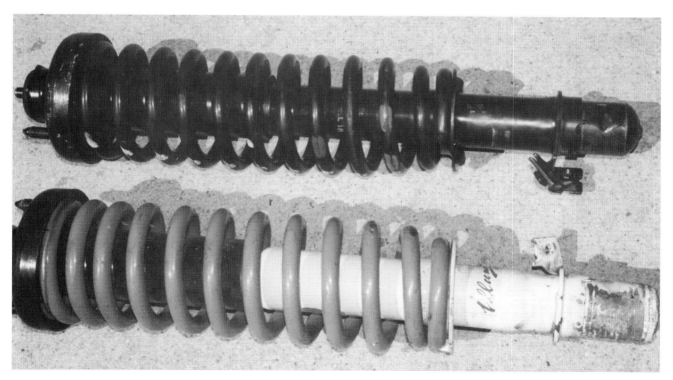

Progress Sport Springs and Tokico Illumina shocks replaced the stock spring and strut. *Jeff Cheechov*

Above and top opposite: Three views of the del Sol: Top is stock, lower is stock suspension with Volk 17-inch wheels, and Yokohama A510 ultra-high-performance tires, and opposite shows how Progress Sport Springs and Tokico Illumina shocks lower the car. *Jeff Cheechov*

Three tires were tested on the del Sol. Closest is the Yokohama 008II race compound DOT legal tire, which reached over 1.0 g on the skid pad. Next is the Yokohama A510 ultra-high-performance tire, and the OE tire is in back.

harshness increases a little over the 15-inch tire size, and the slip angle range right at the limit is smaller. The look of the tire is all business and very aggressive. The wheel and tire package is perfect for street driving and especially for canyon blasting when used with the Progress springs and bars and the Tokico shocks. Without the suspension package, the tires cannot do the job and the look leaves something to be desired.

The other package featured the Yokohama 008 R II tire (205/50 R15), which is a DOT legal race-compound tire. It offers superior traction, but the softer rubber compound is not really designed for daily driving. It just wears too rapidly to be practical on the highway. But for the dual-purpose car, a set of the 008's for autocrossing or time trials on the 15-x7-inch DP wheels (35-millimeter offset) is a great way to go.

Overall, the del Sol is a transformed ride. With either Yokohama package, combined with the Progress springs and bars, the Tokico shocks, and the Energy Suspension bushings, a ho-hum street car becomes a terror in any corner you're brave enough to take on.

extract extreme performance. The urethane bushings from Energy Suspension round out the package.

We tested with two tire setups, both from Yokohama. The Yokohama A510 is an awesome tire. We used 205/40 R17 on 17-inch Volks Racing 17-x7-inch wheels (43-millimeter offset). While not up to racing traction levels, this tire offers exceptional grip while still giving you good wear. The very low profile tire sidewall on the A510 offers excellent responsiveness to driver steering inputs, but ride

del Sol Skidpad Tests

Test 1

Suspension: Original

Wheels: original, 14x5 inch

Tires: Bridgestone RE 85 at 30 PSI

Shocks: Stock

Bushings: Energy Suspension

Counterclockwise lap time: 12.75 seconds

Lateral G force: 0.784

Clockwise lap time: 13.20 seconds

Lateral G force: 0.731

Average: 0.758 g

Comments: The car has excessive body roll and very little grip over-all. Forgiving but slow.

Test 2

Suspension: Original

Wheels: Volk Racing 17-x7-inch

Tires: Yokohama A510 205/40 R17 shaved to 1/2 tread depth at 36 PSI cold

Shocks: Stock

Bushings: Energy Suspension

Counterclockwise lap time: 12.32 seconds

Lateral G force: 0.839

Clockwise lap time: 12.36 seconds

Lateral G force: 0.834

Average: 0.836g

Comments: More traction. On throttle requires 15 degrees more steering lock than off throttle. On throttle push, off throttle loose. Very stable and predictable, but transitions are abrupt. Maximum lateral traction is in a narrow slip angle range due to less than 100 percent tire contact with road surface in corners. Even more body roll due to increased traction.

Test 3

Suspension: Original

Wheels: DP Racing 15-x7-inch

Tires: Yokohama 008 RS II 205/50 R15 at 36 PSI cold

Shocks: Stock

Bushings: Energy Suspension

Counterclockwise lap time: 11.78 seconds

Lateral G force: 0.918

Clockwise lap time: 12.05 seconds

Lateral G force: 0.877

Average: 0.898g

Comments: Superior grip; very predictable; easier to drive at limit. Lateral acceleration over broader range of slip angles due to taller sidewall construction.

Test 4

Suspension: Progress springs, stock bar

Wheels: Volk Racing 17-x7-inch

Tires: Yokohama A510 205/40 R17 shaved to 1/2 inch depth at 36 PSI cold

Shocks: Tokico Illumina

Bushings: Energy suspension

Counterclockwise lap time: 11.79 seconds

Lateral G force: 0.917

Clockwise lap time: 11.84 seconds

Lateral G force: 0.909

Average: 0.913g

Comments: The springs have transformed the car. More traction, more forgiving, more predictable, and easier to drive. Car is neutral and balance left to right is very good. Still too much body roll.

Test 5

Suspension: Progress springs

Wheels: DP Racing 15-x7-inch

Tires: YOKOHAMA 008 RS II 205/50 R15 at 36 PSI cold

Shocks: Tokico Illumina

Bushings: Energy suspension

Counterclockwise lap time: 11.41 seconds

Lateral G force: 0.979

Clockwise lap time: 11.70 seconds

Lateral G force: 0.931

Average: 0.954g

Comments: Excellent grip, but even more roll, which limits tire contact with the road and costs traction. Well balanced and fast.

Test 6

Suspension: Progress springs and front/rear antiroll bars

Wheels: Volk Racing 17-x7-inch

Tires: Yokohama A510 205/40 R17 shaved to 1/2 inch depth at 36 PSI cold

Shocks: Tokico Illumina

Bushings: Energy Suspension

Counterclockwise lap time: 11.52 seconds

Lateral G force: 0.960

Clockwise lap time: 11.77 seconds

Lateral G force: 0.920

Average: 0.940g

Comments: The bars reduced body roll and helped keep the tire contact patch planted and working. This tire combination offers good grip (nearly as fast as the 008's without the front and rear bars) and improved wear over the "R" compound 008 R II.

The Progress crew makes one of several changes to the del Sol during testing.

Test 7

Suspension: Progress springs and front/rear antiroll bars

Wheels: DP Racing 15-x-7-inch

Tires: Yokohama 008 RS II 205/50 R15 at 36 PSI cold

Shocks: Tokico Illumina

Bushings: Energy Suspension

Counterclockwise lap time: 11.18 seconds

Lateral G force: 1.019

Clockwise lap time: 11.25 seconds

Lateral G force: 1.007

Average: 1.013 g

Comments: Very fast, predictable, and balanced. Virtually no difference in left versus right turns.

1993 Honda Accord Street Car

The 1993 Accord is a great daily driver, but honestly, in stock trim it's a little on the ho-hum side. To improve the looks and performance and make the car more fun to drive, new wheels and tires and a sport suspension package were in order. We decided to take the modifications in steps to better monitor the performance improvements. Since this car is a daily driver with most of the performance driving in the mountains and on winding canyon roads, we wanted to create the best compromise between fun performance and comfort. Looks are a factor, but a back-wrenching ride is not acceptable.

Our goal is to improve handling performance as well as looks, so we wanted a 17-inch wheel. We decided to push the envelope as far as possible with wheel and tire sizing, so we used

The 1993 Honda Accord makes a great project car, responding exceptionally to suspension changes.

the Rial 17x8-inch-wide six-spoke aluminum wheels imported by Wheel Dynamix in Florida. Rial is a German wheel maker with a reputation for quality and light weight. Weight is an

The Progress Sport Springs lower the Accord about 2 inches from stock and increase the spring rates about 60 percent.

The Rial wheels are 17 by 8 inches with Continental ContiSport 215/40 ZR17 ultra-high-performance tires.

issue on wheels, since lighter wheels reduce unsprung weight and that reduces ride harshness. Since the short tire sidewall on the 17-inch wheels will make the ride stiffer, the lightweight wheels should counteract this, leaving us with good ride quality.

On the clean-looking Rials, we mounted a set of Toyo Proxes T1-Plus 215-45 ZR17 tires, which is Toyo's stickiest ultra-high-performance street radial. This is a plus-2 increase in the tire, but the rolling circumference is less than 0.25 inches smaller than stock. This a big tire and wheel combination for this platform, but we want to see how it does.

Finding the best compromise for the street takes sound engineering. We started with the wheels and tires only, with stock suspension. The car sits way too high to look right, but this is a work in progress, not the finished product.

The Toyo Proxes T1-Plus tires offer huge increases in grip over the OEM tires. With a 215-45 ZR17 tire size on an 8-inch-wide wheel, the traction potential increases by about one-third over the OEM tires, but only if the suspension controls the tire contact patches properly. In performance and safety terms, this means higher cornering speeds and shorter stopping distances. If you're canyon blasting, autocrossing, or time trialing, the car is

The Accord looks great lowered about 2 inches from stock. The Rial wheels and ContiSport tires add to the looks and the performance.

faster. If you're attempting to avoid the dweeb who just crashed in front of you, you stand a better chance of exiting the situation unscathed.

With the stock ride height and soft suspension, the performance increase did not match the potential offered by the wheel/tire combination. But it's still a major improvement, as the skid pad times show, with a two-

direction average of 0.844 gs. This says a lot about stock Honda handling and the Toyo Proxes T1-plus tires.

Even though the car looks a little dorky with all that air between the tire and the fender well, and the body roll is excessive at the cornering limit, you'd never know it from behind the wheel. The car already feels much better in the corners and under braking. Steering response is better, traction is greater, and even the handling balance is in the high-performance ballpark.

At the limits of traction during cornering, the car exhibits slight understeer. By lifting off the throttle in a corner, slight trailing throttle oversteer kicks in, helping to negate the basic steady state understeer. Lowering the car with sport springs, adding performance shocks, and fitting larger antiroll bars should help make the car more neutral at the limit and more responsive during corner turn-in, both elements of performance handling. The 0.844 g lateral acceleration average for laps in both directions is far better than the below 0.80 gs from the stock wheel/tire combo, but well below the potential of the Toyo Proxes T1-Plus tires.

Even though performance is better, all is not perfect. The aggressive wheel/tire sizing causes the tires to protrude from the fender wells slightly. Under extreme cornering, when encountering a significant bump, slight rubbing of the tire

Energy Suspension makes a complete set of bushings for the 1993 Accord, including antiroll bar bushings and end links, control arm bushings, and strut mount bushings, all of which contribute to improved responsiveness without increasing harshness and noise too much.

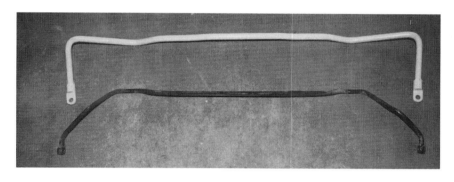

The Progress rear antiroll bar is much more substantial than the stock unit (black), increasing rear roll resistance and improving the handling balance dramatically.

The Progress rear spring and the Tokico Illumina shock absorber made a substantial improvement in overall handling.

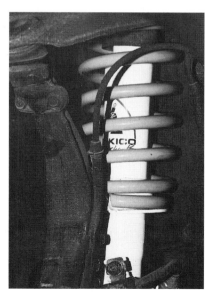

The front Progress Sport Spring lowers the car about 2 inches and the Tokico Illumina strut insert is adjustable in rebound allowing transient handling to be easily tuned.

A 205/55 R15 Kumho Ecsta Supra 712 ultra-high-performance tire mounted on the Accord's stock wheels.

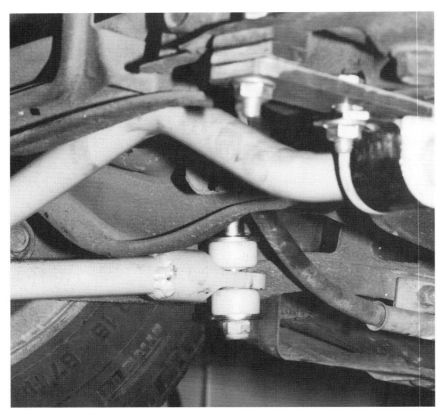

The Progress rear antiroll bar requires an additional mounting bracket for installation.

against the outside rear fender well occurs. It's not a major problem, but it must be addressed.

The next step was to install Progress Sport Springs and a rear antiroll bar (see the installation sidebar). The Progress springs are significantly stiffer than stock with a rate increase of 58 percent in the front and 63 percent in the rear. The ride height is lowered by about 1.75 to 2.0 inches. While stiffer, ride comfort is completely acceptable for a daily driver even on bumpy roads.

We installed Tokico Illumina shocks at the same time. These shocks are rebound adjustable and increase damping just the right amount for the more aggressive springs. The adjustments on the rebound side allow more aggressive settings when the mood strikes and you can fine-tune the transient handling balance for the occasional autocross or track day.

The package retained the stock front bar but replaced the rear bar with

Installing the suspension on our Honda Accord project car was relatively simple. The installation takes about three hours with hand tools. The front suspension requires realignment after installation is complete.

The front strut assembly requires removal and a spring compressor is needed to remove the old spring and shock insert to make way for the new Progress Sport Springs and Tokico Illumina shocks.

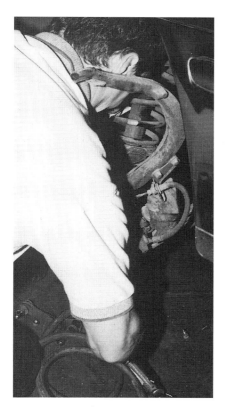

The rear spring and shock are a little easier to remove than the front.

a much larger piece that is designed to create a near neutral handling balance. The look of the car is transformed and so is the responsiveness. The car feels much more nimble, the roll couple (handling balance) is very neutral with mild power-on understeer and a touch of trailing throttle oversteer when you lift abruptly off the throttle in mid-turn. Very nice.

With the stock wheels and tires, the tire grip shows a remarkable improvement. Cornering force increased to the level of the big Toyo Proxes T1Plus tires. The grip increased even more with the Toyos on the Rial wheels, but the rubbing problem at the rear also increased to an unacceptable level. The front is fine, but the wheel offset and width at the rear combined with the tire height is too great to clear the fenderwell.

To cure the problem we installed a set of Continental Sport Contact 215/40R17 tires on the Rial 17-x8-inch wheels. The clearance problems were cured, and Continentals provided exceptional responsiveness though cornering and braking grip were very slightly reduced compared to the Toyo T1Plus. Grip was nearly the same with skid pad average cornering force of 0.932 gs, less than a hundredth of a g off the time of the Toyo T1 Plus tires. Driveability is improved and street performance is phenomenal, especially on winding canyon and mountain roads. This initial experience with the Continental Sport Contact was a pleasant surprise. And all indications are that this tire will offer excellent wear, especially considering the grip level and great responsiveness to driver steering inputs.

The final modification to the Accord was a set of Energy Suspension bushings. We wanted to do this last to really test the difference in responsiveness and feel. The bushings actually increase grip a small amount because the reduced compliance reduces camber change at the front and helps keep the tire contact patch flat on the road surface.

The reduced compliance in the suspension is also noticeable in the way

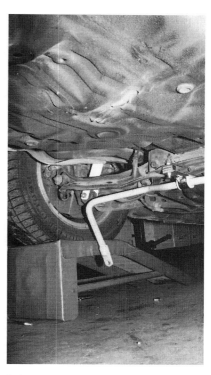

A larger rear antiroll bar was installed to improve roll couple distribution and reduce the Accord's inherent understeer.

the car reacts to steering inputs. The response is quicker and the feel is more positive. The ride harshness also increases, but only slightly and it's worth the improved feel and response. This makes the bushing kit a very cost-effective addition to the suspension system.

For a small investment in wheels, tires, and suspension, the 1993 Accord now corners as well as a BMW M3. The ride is firm but comfortable, the responsiveness is greatly improved, the car looks better, and the cornering force is significantly better. Braking performance is also improved and it all improves the safety of the car.

The Progress Sport package with the Tokico Illumina shocks, the Energy Suspension polyurethane bushings, and the Continental Sport Contact 215/40R17 tires on the Rial 17x8-inch wheel proved to be an excellent compromise. And it's way more fun to drive, which was our original goal.

147

Chapter Seventeen
Subaru Project Car

2001 Subaru WRX

Not since the 1960s has a factory hot rod such as the Subaru Impreza WRX been offered to the U.S. market. But this case, the inspiration comes from rallying, not drag racing. That translates into a road car with exceptional cornering, braking, and acceleration. And all-wheel drive means the high level of performance is not just for fair-weather sport. The WRX can tackle any weather and road conditions that the most daring driver is willing to go for.

Two factors separate the WRX from nearly all other performance road cars, at least those under $100,000. The suspension and chassis are very

The Subaru WRX is at its best on windy, mountain roads. The WRX has one of the most aggressive suspension systems among production sedans available in the U.S.

While basesd on the World rally Championship car, the WRX would perform better and look better with a lowered suspension. In spite of that, the car's handling is exceptional right off the showroom floor.

aggressive, and the handling balance of the car is superb. Just a hint of power-on understeer balanced nicely with a bit of trailing throttle oversteer. But best of all, the all-wheel drive on the WRX combined with excellent torque and power means the car is a rocket off the turns. Corner exit is the key to fast driving on winding roads, autocross courses, road courses, and rally roads. The WRX is a perfect package for getting out of corners as fast as possible.

We tested the stock 2001 WRX with the optional BBS 7-x17-inch wheel package and Bridgestone Potenza RE 011 ultra-high-perform-ance tires. Otherwise, the car was com-pletely stock, though that term is used very loosely with this car. From an

The sport package option includes BBS 17 x 7 wheels and 205/50R17 Bridgestone Potenza RE011 tires.

aggression perspective, the WRX is at least on par with other projects in this book, like the turbo Golf and array of Hondas. While the ride is not overly harsh, it is firmer than one would expect from a stock vehicle. Cornering speeds, handling balance, braking, and corner exit acceleration are superb, with sound engineering across the board. Right off the showroom floor, the WRX will handle as well as most cars modified with a well-engineered suspension and wheel/tire package. That says a lot about the engineering philosophy of the Subaru engineers.

The packaging of the WRX is clearly based on the World rally and SCCA rally cars. For improved performance on highways, autocross, and road courses, lowering the ride height of the car 2 to 3 inches would help, plus it would improve the looks. But for rallying on rough roads, the setup is ideal.

The chassis feels rigid during limit cornering. The overall strength of the suspension and chassis is also felt on interstates, where noise and vibration are higher than one would expect from a stock vehicle. But that is a small price to pay for the improved performance the chassis rigidity brings.

Braking is excellent, even from high speed. Upgraded rotors and pads would improve braking even more. The balance of the car allows trail braking fairly deep into a corner. The transition from braking to balanced cornering is smooth with a small throttle application.

At the limit, the car shows basic understeer if over driven at turn-in, but quickly lift off the throttle and the car will oversteer slightly, pointing the nose into the turn apex and allowing a quick return to some amount of open throttle depending on the turn radius. As soon as you begin to unwind the steering, more throttle can be applied. Full throttle can be applied relatively early exiting a turn, earlier than one expects from

Above and opposite: These two views show the strut front suspension of the WRX.

a turbo-equipped car. The exit acceleration is exceptional and clearly the strongest point of the WRX. The platform could handle substantial power increases without flinching.

On smoother roads, the ride is good. Over bumps, you feel the stiffness of the suspension and the rigidity of the chassis, but it is not excessive. On interstates with wearing expansion strips, the WRX bucks at 70 to 80 miles per hour. This is as much a statement about the wearing interstate system in some locations as it is about the aggressive nature of the WRX suspension. The level of road noise on concrete at highway speed is also high, but not so on asphalt. Again, this is partly due to the nature of the WRX, the tire tread design, and road surface.

The rear suspension the WRX features parallel lower coontrol links.

The BBS wheels are not only stunning to look at, but very rigid as well, which helps the feel of the WRX during cornering. The Bridgestone Potenza RE 011 tires offer excellent grip in the dry, typical of an ultra-high-performance tire. But like other high-end Potenzas, the RE 011 design is somewhat flexible, which improves ride quality but slows the response to driver steering inputs at corner turn-in. This is not really noticed on slow- and medium-speed turns since the wheel is turned both farther and more quickly. But in high-speed turns, where steering inputs are smaller and slower, it is noticeable. This is not really a problem and does not affect performance, but it takes a little adjustment to driving style to compensate for this tendency. Beyond that, the tires are excellent.

The WRX provides excellent performance right out of the showroom. But for the serious handling enthusiast, a set of coil-overs to adjust ride heights for track and rally situations and a set of tires for each discipline, and the WRX would be the ultimate multipurpose performance vehicle.

Chapter Eighteen
Volkswagen Project Cars

NASA Neuspeed GTi Cup

Formula 1 teams spend about $200 million a season, and NASCAR teams about $10 million. Even the independents in the SCCA Speedvision World Challenge spend up to $100,000 for a 10-race season. Well, don't delete your racing dreams yet. How about a $3,000 racecar that you can run for a 10-race season for under $4,000 plus travel expenses. And points money is even awarded at season's end.

By taking an inexpensive used car, creating a set of rules that enhance performance but keep costs low, making the car really easy to build and cheap to race, the National Auto Sport Association (NASA) has come up with what has to be the

cheapest way to go road racing anywhere. The line is that a car can be built for as low as $3,000—ready to race! And a weekend of racing will cost less than $400 plus travel expenses. That includes tires, racecar fuel, basic maintenance, and entry fees. Crash damage, which is rare in NASA, is extra. And at NASA events, a weekend of racing usually includes two practice/qualifying sessions and a race each day. That's nearly three hours of track time per weekend. And they allow two drivers to share a car for a weekend, so costs can be reduced even further. NASA conducts a series of endurance races ranging from 3 hours to the Timex 12 Hour. The GTi Cup cars can run in the

enduros, and you can share expenses with other drivers.

NASA is a growing association, with a strong program in northern California and Arizona, and growing programs in southern California, Nevada, Virginia, and the Midwest. The GTi also fits into the SCCA Improved Touring B class, though a stock engine will not allow the car to run up front if any competition shows up. You can also autocross the car, run in time trials, even rally it if the mood strikes. And import drag racing in a bracket class would be a gas, although a slow one. If you don't mind the most Spartan of environments, you could even drive the car on the street. Talk about an all-around vehicle. So, just

The race car's body roll is minimal and rear roll stiffness is high enough eliminate understeer. The inside rear tire just lifts off the track surface in a corner at the limits of traction.

what do you need to get involved? We'll start with the rules and what it takes to build the basic car.

Rules Overview

Inexpensive racing? It can be when you start with a 16-plus-year-old economy car that costs in the $1,000 range for a decent example, and combine that with smart rules.

Let's start with the car. Any Volkswagen Rabbit from 1975 to 1984 is eligible. Earlier cars in this range can be updated to 1983–1984 GTi models by using the 1.8-liter, 8.5:1 compression, solid lifter engine. While older models may be really cheap, finding a 1983–1984 GTi in good shape will save some time and expense. You will need the 1.8-liter engine to be competitive, and swapping one in an older car is easy, but just an extra step.

The basic engine rule is "run it stock." You can rebuild, but only stock parts are allowed. You can balance the engine, but no blueprinting, port matching, or cam profiling. The idea is to keep it cheap, easy, and—most of all—fun. The sanctioning body, NASA, can claim (as in "take your engine") engines from any competitor for $500 if officials feel that a racer is cheating. If that happens, you go buy a new engine and start over. Good junkyard motors cost in the $200 range, so you're not out bucks, just time, unless of course you have spent big money or weeks of effort building an engine.

Once they have the claimed engine, they tear it down. If it's legal, NASA sells the parts, likely to the competition. Illegal parts are destroyed; the culprit is disqualified and loses points for the race and the season. Stiff penalties, but the idea is to keep it simple, cheap, and fun. If you want to build race engines, pick another class.

The only things you can change are spark plugs, plug wires, filters, oil pan, windage tray, and oil lines. You can add an oil cooler. The fuel injection must be stock CIS units from 1977 to 1984 cars. Only the fuel mix-

The stock car was in good shape, but looked a little outdated. With lowered suspension, big tires and graphics, the 1983 GTi will look more contemporary and perform far beyond the investment.

ture can be altered by modifying the resistance valves that feed the injector. The throttle linkage may be changed or modified.

The interior can be stripped of carpet, headliner, and sound deadening insulation. Radios, speakers, heater, and air conditioner can be removed. Sunroofs can be replaced with sheet metal securely fastened to the roof. The driver's seat, steering wheel, and shift knob can be replaced with racing parts.

Some modifications are *required*. The front brake rotors must be vented rotors from a 1983–1984 GTi. Brake pads must be Hawk Blue compound. Springs, antiroll bars, upper and lower tie bars, and bushings must be Neuspeed. Shocks are Bilstein. The shifter, motor mounts, and K & N filter are optional. Wheels must be stock alloy or steel, 6-x14-inch, and the spec tire is the Toyo Proxes RA-1 in the 205/55-14 size. Other small modifications will be outlined as we proceed with the buildup.

The First Step

Obtaining a car is clearly the first thing to do. We spent about two months looking in newspapers and the

Internet for a GTi, finding one by word of mouth about 150 miles north of Los Angeles. The car is a silver 1983 GTi with low (relatively) mileage (160,000+), fairly straight body, and good engine/driveline. After test driving the car and checking it over, we paid $850. The price included some spare parts, inluding rotors, a grille, tie rods, bushings, and some miscellaneous parts, as well as some needed for the conversion to a racecar. The car needed some minor body repairs, a new windshield, paint, and the required parts to make a beater into a racer.

Getting Started

The work began by completely stripping the interior of the car. This is easy, but time-consuming work. The hardest part was removing all of the gooey sound-deadening and insulation material. We also removed the heater and air conditioner and associated hardware from under the dash and the engine compartment. This would make it possible to get the race weight down to the minimum of 2,150 pounds with the driver.

Next, we acquired a roll cage kit from Autopower. This kit proved to

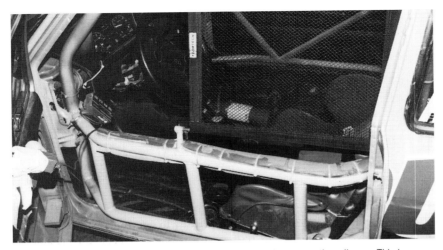

From the driver's side door, the NASCAR-style door bars can beseen on the roll cage. This improves safety, but requires gutting all but the door latch mechanism from the driver's door, legal if you use the NASCAR door bars.

be an excellent design with everything fitting perfectly. We welded the cage in and added a couple of bars that are legal in NASA rules but not part of the kit. This included NASCAR-style

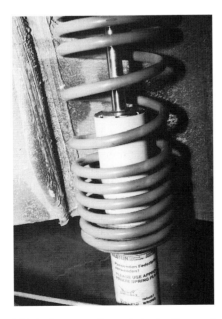

This is the rear spring and shock. Neuspeed sport springs and Bilstein gas pressure shocks form the basis for the GTi Cup racer. The lower spring perch fits in a groove on the shock body. Multiple grooves allow ride height adjustments at the rear to fine-tune crossweight percentage and handling balance.

door bars on the driver side to increase driver safety. Brackets were welded to the cage for the window net, and the fabrication work was complete. The racing seat and driver restraints were mounted and the dash reinstalled with most of the original gauges removed. Except for paint, the interior was completed.

It took only a few hours to install Neuspeed springs and Bilstein shocks. The antiroll bars and strut braces from Neuspeed were even easier to install. This was all simple bolt-on equipment. We also installed new Hawk brake pads as required and purged and bled the brake system and filled the system with racing high-temperature brake fluid.

At this point, we checked everything out, including CV joints, wheel bearings, transmission, and engine. The original engine had good compression, but we knew a rebuild was likely in the near future. Everything was in good enough shape to test the car and run a race or two before replacing original parts.

After the initial testing, we started on the minor bodywork and painting. This was by far the worst part of turning the GTi into a racecar. The bodywork, sanding, painting, and graphics application took more time than the rest of the project combined. Most of what we did

was not really necessary, especially the graphics, but we decided it was worth the effort to make the car look good.

After the paint was on the car, we added a front air dam to reduce drag and give the rabbit some much needed front downforce to improve medium- to high-speed cornering. Next we tackled the setup.

We put the car on the scales, hoping that we would be under the 2,150-pound minimum weight. We were under by about 50 pounds, so we added ballast to the car in the most desirable location within the restraints of the NASA rules. Our goal was to get the right side weight as close to the left side weight as possible for equal cornering power left to right. We also wanted to get more weight to the rear, more difficult due to the ballast placement restrictions. Our corner weights with 5 gallons of fuel looked like this:

Left front	736
Right front	681
Left rear	409
Right rear	350

Total weight = 2,176 pounds

Left side = 1,145 pounds or 52.6 percent

Front = 1,417 pounds or 65.1 percent

Crossweight (RF+LR) = 1,090 pounds

Crossweight percent (RF+LR/total weight) = 50.09 percent

This was without adjusting any ride height on any corner of the car. The cross-weight is perfect, the left side is good, and the front is too high but as low as we can possibly get and stay at the lowest legal weight. This is the easiest corner weight setup I've ever seen.

Next we checked the alignment. Caster was right on the factory specs, and we checked toe with a tape measure, but very carefully. The front had less than 1/16 inch of toe-out, while the rear had something less than 1/8 inch of toe-in. We decided to get a more accurate reading using the ART Laser Toe gauge. The front toe-out was 0.045 inches, less than 3/64 of an inch, a great starting point. The rear toe-in measured at 0.071 inches, just under 1/16 inch, also an excellent starting point. Bump steer looked good, but steering modifications are not allowed so we decided not to worry about it. It proved to be no problem on the track. Camber looked OK, but it would be adjusted as needed at the track based on tire temperature data. Tire pressures were set a 35 psi in the Toyo Proxes RA-1 tires. We were ready to load the Rabbit on the trailer for its first track excursion.

After torquing the wheel bolts and checking the tire pressures, the first track test was at hand. The car felt very skittish, even after the tires warmed. It had some understeer, but lacked grip in general. A quick trip to the pit lane to check tire temperatures was called for. The temps provided the answers. Too much heat in the centers of all of the tires, meaning that the tires were overinflated.

We lowered the front pressures to 30 psi and the rears to 25 psi. The car then felt totally different: good grip and only a slight push in slower corners. Another check of the tire temps showed the fronts still a little too hot in the center of the tread and the rears generally cooler than the fronts. We dropped the front tire pressure by 1 pound and the rears by 3 pounds, and the car was nearly perfect.

Like every other phase of the setup, this car was a breeze. Neuspeed has done a masterful job of creating a well-balanced package that makes the car easy to set up and even easier to drive. Cornering force is high, well over 1.0-g. Braking is good and tire wear excellent. Overall a great package.

During the first outing, we decided we needed to add front brake ducting to reduce possible brake fade, which was minor but could get worse on a really hot day. We had already replaced the old fluid with Motul Racing High

Temp brake fluid, and it worked very well. We also noticed that the transmission felt a little weak in third gear. But our lap times were competitive right away at Buttonwillow Raceway Park, so overall we were very pleased.

At our first race, we had some electrical problems and at the second race event, the fuel injector nozzles acted up. We solved the electrical problems and got a couple of second-place finishes at the first event, but at the second event, the injectors needed replacing, so we went home early. We went to Willow Springs to test the replaced injectors and the car ran very strong, at least until the transmission popped out of third gear about 100 rpm before the third to fourth shift. The engine over-revved and tagged some valves. A compression check confirmed this with three of four cylinders way down on compression. So the drivetrain came out and the engine was sent to VW Specialties for a rebuild.

The VW Specialties rebuild, which included valves, a valve job, rings, bearings, gaskets, and labor cost less than $1,000. We also installed a Neuspeed Quick Shift kit to cure the shifting problem. After a track test, the engine was stronger than ever and the shifting problems disappeared. We now expect the engine and transmission to last for about 30 events, about three seasons of racing. We anticipate replacing the CV joints and wheel bearings at the end of the current season.

The car took about 200 man-hours to build, and the cost of all of the parts, including paint but not the graphics (paid for by a sponsor) and a set of Toyo RA-1 tires was less than $3,100. Add the cost of the car and it was less than $4,000 to build a race-ready car that is competitive.

Brake pads cost about $20 per weekend and the Toyo Proxes RA-1 DOT race tires at $550 a set, average about seven weekends or 20 hours of track time. The cost is $27 per hour or about $80 per weekend event. Oil

changes are about $30 every two events ($15 per event) and fuel use is about 20 gallons a weekend. Even using $5 per gallon racing fuel, fuel will cost $100 per event. The total cost, not counting entry fees, is about $275 per weekend. That is a very inexpensive way to go road racing. Entry fees range from $250 to $300 per event.

In the final analysis, the GTi Cup car is great fun to drive, and at some races 20 cars will be in attendance, so there is lots of competition. The cars are easy to setup and maintain, and the cost is very reasonable for the amount of fun.

Volkswagen New Beetle Cup Racecar

From a distance the Beetle Cup cars look like Beetles. And they are, but far from what you can buy off the showroom. Fully tweaked by Volkswagen Racing in Germany, the Beetle Cup cars start life as a bare shell. A full roll cage structure is added to provide driver safety and a rigid platform. The VR6 V-6 engine is mated to a six-speed gearbox and wedged into the engine bay. The 2.8-liter engine produces 204 horsepower and 200 foot pounds of torque with a 6,800-rpm redline. The engines are basically stock but blueprinted and dyno-tuned to within 1.5 horsepower of each other.

The suspension features H & R Sport Springs and Bilstein shocks. The four-piston front calipers are from ATE Racing, with front antilock system and 355-millimeter vented rotors with stock rear calipers and 232-millimeter solid ATE rotors. Wheels are 18-x9-inch O.Z. Superturisimo with Pirelli 235/625-18 slicks (or racing rain tires). The weight without driver is 2,579 pounds. The body modifications include a front air dam with air inlets for cooling and brake ducts. The rear wing adds downforce, and the rear bumper cover helps air exit from under the car at speed. Safety equipment includes an OMP driver-restraint system and racing seat.

The New Beetle Cup cars are very sophisticated racers with little body roll and perfect handling balance. The 20 identical cars created an exceptional racing environment at Road Atlanta. *Franczak Ent./Volkswagen*

Driving the Cup cars is a gas. The cars are perfectly balanced when the big Pirelli stickies are hot. On cold tires there is a hint of understeer. The cars will decelerate at nearly 1.2 gs and corner in excess of 1.1 gs, real racecar numbers. The cars are very stable at speed (we were reaching nearly 130 miles per hour before the downhill braking zone at Road Atlanta's turn 10a) and under braking. The rear wing provides downforce, which I learned while drafting three cars into turn 10a under braking. The turbulence took air off my rear wing and rear brake lockup made the car wiggle, while alone at the same spot the car was perfect. Although you can catch other cars in the draft, passing is nearly impossible as the aero drag slows the car as soon as you pull alongside the other car by about one-third car length.

2000 Neuspeed Golf 1.8 Turbo

Some cars just look right from the moment you lay eyes on them. Neuspeed has a well deserved reputation for creating first-class project cars, and the 2000 Golf 1.8 Turbo is no exception. For nearly 30 years,

Neuspeed has been making parts for Volkswagens and more recently a selection of other cars. Our Rabbit GTi Cup project uses Neuspeed gear, and it works exceptionally well. The Golf project is no different. The 1.8 Turbo is very aggressive in the suspension department for street driving, but

everything works well together. Though the ride is on the harsh side, if you want exceptional performance from a car that can be driven to work and the grocery store as well as on an autocross course or race track, the Neuspeed Golf is a very cost effective way to go.

Starting with the suspension, the Golf is equipped with the Neuspeed/Bilstein adjustable coil-over suspension, which includes the excellent Bilstein gas pressure struts and shocks and Neuspeed's coil-over springs. A Neuspeed front 25-millimeter antiroll bar and a Neuspeed rear 28-millimeter adjustable antiroll bar increase roll resistance significantly. The adjustable rear bar allows fine-tuning roll couple distribution, giving the owner the option of a slightly tighter setup for the road and a more aggressive neutral setup for the track. The rod end links for both front and rear antiroll bars allow easy adjustment to eliminate pre-load and quick changes to the rear bar to adjust balance. Polyurethane suspension bushings round out the suspension mods on the Golf.

A Neuspeed billet aluminum front lower tie bar, Neuspeed front upper

The Golf looks impressive lowered on the 18–x-8-inch Volk wheels and BFG g-Force T/A KD ultra-high-performance tires.

strut tie bar and a Neuspeed billet aluminum front lower tie bar are used to improve chassis rigidity and vehicle responsiveness. Neuspeed stainless steel brake lines are used to improve pedal feel and braking responsiveness for the Audi TT Sport brake kit featuring 12.3-inch front slotted rotors and 10.0-inch ventilated/slotted rear rotors. Volk Racing SE37 forged aluminum 8-x18-inch wheels, and BF Goodrich G-Force TA KD tires 245/40R18 provide the large footprint for high levels of traction.

Neuspeed billet aluminum polished front lower grille, oil cap, power steering cap, strut tower caps, and coolant capalong with Bosch HID headlamps, European front and rear bumpers, 4-Motion front spoiler, and rear valance were added to improve the looks and add finish detail to the package.

Engine performance of the 1.8 Turbo is seriously enhanced by the addition of a Neuspeed P-Flo air intake, a Neuspeed Hi-Flow turbo air intake pipe, a Neuspeed P-Chip ECU modification, and a Neuspeed T304 2.25-inch stainless steel cat-back exhaust. The combination of these parts improves power output to the 220 brake horsepower range. A Neuspeed short shift kit makes shifting very quick and precise.

The first improvement striking the senses when you light the Golf is the sweet exhaust tone. While the power improvement is most important, the exhaust note adds to the feel and joy of the car. The second feature grabbing your attention is the short, positive throw of the shifter. Again, the performance improvement is key, but the feel really indicates that you are about to embark on a serious drive.

And that feeling of a serious ride amps up a notch or two as soon as you pull out of the driveway. Everything from the tire contact patch through the suspension and chassis feels very firm. And it is. It's hard to be patient waiting for the first on-ramp to get a real feel

The strut tower brace adds rigidity. The Neuspeed engine tweaks increase power output to nearly 220 horsepower.

for the grip. The wait is worth it, but you quickly find that the level of handling performance and grip is much higher than expected.

It took some time behind the wheel on seriously winding roads to tell that the setup created a small degree of understeer. This is with the rear antiroll bar in the middle setting, and is perfect for driving windy roads and interstate ramps. The stiffest rear antiroll bar setting is ideal for autocrossing or serious track driving on a track day. The other surprise is the braking performance. The braking is so good at the limit that you tend to brake way too early for a turn until you become very familiar with the braking force. When driving on city streets, the brakes grab a little during light applications. The Audi-based package is great for hard driving but a little too aggressive for normal driving at low speeds. But after repeated hard deceleration on mountain roads, the brake system showed no signs of fade, a major positive for aggressive driving on road or track.

While the overall suspension and braking systems are exceptional, the cornerstone of the great performance is the BFG g-Force KD ultra-high-performance tire. These tires are simply outstanding in all aspects of driv-

ing. Grip is very high. We did not slalom, skid pad, or brake test this car, but the cornering force was easily in the 0.95 g range and the responsiveness to steering inputs indicates that this package would be near 70 miles per hour on a 700-foot slalom. Braking performance is also impressive, with estimated stops from 60 miles per hour in less than 115 feet.

While the traction of the BFG KD tire is superb, even more impressive is the feel of this tire. It is very responsive to driver steering inputs, but more important, it is completely linear in its feel and totally predictable. This is a tire that never fools you by unloading at the wrong time or taking too long to take a set going into a corner. While this tire likes to be driven smoothly for peak performance, it is forgiving if you are overly aggressive with the steering or brakes.

One of the true signs of a great performing front-wheel-drive car with substantial horsepower is the car's reaction to corner exit acceleration. High levels of traction translate into hard acceleration with no hint of wheel spin in medium- to high-speed corners. The car exhibits no hint of torque steer, and only the slowest of hairpin turns requires judicious throttle pedal applications.

Resources

Advanced Racing Technologies, Inc.
17 North Cross Road
Staatsburg, NY 12580 USA
Tel/Fax: 914-889-4499
Web: advancedracing.com
Email: AdvancedRacing@compuserve.com

Autopower
3424 Pickett Street
San Diego, CA 92110
Tel: 619-297-3300
Fax: 619-297-9765

Autotech Sport Tuning
33240-E Paseo Adelanto
San Juan Capistrano, CA 92675
Tel: 800-553-1055
Fax: 949-240-0450
Web: www.autotech.com

BF Goodrich Tires
P.O. Box 19001
Greenville, SC 29602-9001
Web: www.bfgoodrichtires.com

Bilstein Shock Absorbers
Tel: 800-537-1085
Web: www.bilstein.com

Brembo Brakes
1585 Sunflower Avenue
Costa Mesa, CA 92626-1532
Tel: 714-641-5831
Fax: 714-641-5827
Web: www.brembo.com

Continental Tires
1800 Continental Boulevard
Charlotte, NC 28273
Tel: 800-743-7075
Web: www.contigentire.com

Eibach Springs
17817 Gillette Avenue
Irvine, CA 92614-6501
Tel: 949-752-6700
Fax: 949-752-6788
Web: www.eibach.com

Energy Suspension
1131 via Callejon
San Clemente, CA 92673
Tel: 949-367-3935
Fax: 949-361-3940
Web: www.energysuspension.com

Fastlane Racing School
P.O. Box 220192
Santa Clarita, CA 91322
Tel: 888-948-4888
Fax: 661-287-4371
Web: www.raceschool.com
E-mail: fastlaneinfo@aol.com

General Tires
1800 Continental Boulevard
Charlotte, NC 28273
Tel: 800-743-7075
Web: www.contigentire.com

Ground Control
Tel: 530-677-8600
Fax: 530-677-9090
Web: www.ground-control.com

H & R Springs
3815 Bakerview Spur #7
Bellingham, WA 98226
Tel: 360-738-8881
Fax: 360-738-8889
Web: www.hrsprings.com

Hoosier Tires
65465 U.S. 31
Lakeville, IN 46536
Tel: 219-784-3152
Fax: 219-784-2385
Web: www.hoosiertire.com

Hotchkis Tuning
12035 Burke Street, Suite 13
Santa Fe Springs, CA 90670
Tel: 562-907-7757
Fax : 562-907-7765
www.hotchkistuning.com

Koni Shocks
1961A International Way
Hebron, KY 41048
Tel: 800-994-KONI
Web: www.koni-na.com

Kumho Tires
Tel: 800-HiKumho
Web: www.kumhotireusa.com

M/C Tech Motorsports
13600 Quinnault, Unit #8
Apple Valley, CA 92307
Tel: 760-240-5083

Neuspeed
3300 Corte Malpaso
Camarillo, CA 93012
Tel: 805-388-7171
Fax: 805-388-0030
Web: www.neuspeed.com

Progress Group
1390 N. Hundley Street
Anaheim, CA 92806
Tel: 714-575-1193
Fax: 714-575-1198
Web: www.progressauto.com

Tire Rack
771 Chippewa Avenue
South Bend, IN 46614
Tel: 888-981-3952
Fax: 219-236-7707
Web: www.tirerack.com

Tokico Shock Absorbers
1330 Storm Parkway
Torrance, CA 90501
Tel: 310-534-4934
Fax: 310-534-2966
Web: www.tokicogasshocks.com

Toyo Tires
6415 Katella Avenue, 2nd Floor
Cypress, CA 90630
Tel: 800-678-3250
Fax: 714-229-6181
Web: www.toyo.com

VW Specialties
17682 Gothard Street, Unit G
Huntington Beach, CA 92646
Tel: 714-848-3766

Wilwood Brakes
4700 Calle Bolero
Camarillo, CA 93012
Tel: 805-388-1188
Fax: 805-987-5982
Web: www.wilwood.com

Yokohama Tires
601 S. Acacia Avenue
Fullerton, CA 92831
Tel: 800-423-4544
Fax: 714-870-3838
Web: www.yokohamatire.com

Index

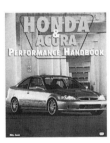

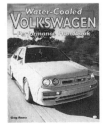